My Heart *in* His Hands

Autumn

I Delight Greatly in My Lord

VONETTE
Zachary
BRIGHT

NewLife
PUBLICATIONS

My Heart in His Hands:
I Delight Greatly in My Lord

Published by
NewLife Publications
A ministry of Campus Crusade for Christ
P.O. Box 620877
Orlando, FL 32862-0877

Production by Genesis Group

Edited by Brenda Josee, Tammy Campbell, Joette Whims, and Lynn Copeland

Cover by Koechel Peterson Design

Printed in the United States of America

ISBN 1-56399-163-2

Unless otherwise indicated, Scripture quotations are from the *New International Version*, © 1973, 1978, 1984 by the International Bible Society. Published by Zondervan Bible Publishers, Grand Rapids, Michigan.

Scripture quotations designated Amplified are from *The Amplified Bible*, © 1965 by Zondervan Publishing House, Grand Rapids, Michigan.

For more information, write:

Campus Crusade for Christ International—100 Lake Hart Drive, Orlando, FL 32832, USA

L.I.F.E., Campus Crusade for Christ—P.O. Box 40, Flemington Markets, 2129, Australia

Campus Crusade for Christ of Canada—Box 529, Sumas, WA 98295

Campus Crusade for Christ—Fairgate House, King's Road, Tyseley, Birmingham, B11 2AA, United Kingdom

Lay Institute for Evangelism, Campus Crusade for Christ—P.O. Box 8786, Auckland, 1035, New Zealand

Campus Crusade for Christ—9 Lock Road #3-03, PacCan Centre, Singapore

Great Commission Movement of Nigeria—P.O. Box 500, Jos, Plateau State, Nigeria, West Africa

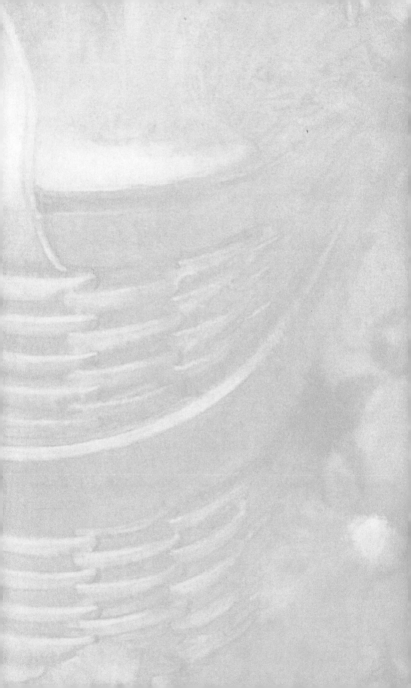

Contents

A Note of Thanks

I love being a woman. My mother made womanhood seem so special. She enjoyed working in the marketplace, but in no way deprived her family. I owe my visions of womanhood to her. My desire as a Christian woman has been not only to present the gospel to all who would listen, but to encourage women to be all they can be. They do this by finding their identity in Jesus Christ and their fulfillment in His plan for their life, then exerting their influence to improve the welfare of their home, community, nation, and the world.

I believe women largely hold the moral key to society. To mobilize them for the cause of Christ, Women Today International was created. Mary Graham, a twenty-seven-year Crusade staff member, co-directed this ministry, helped launch the radio program *Women Today with Vonette Bright*, and served as its producer. The scripts for these daily programs form the basis of this book—daily nuggets to help women find answers and encouragement, cope with circumstances, and realize their significance and influence.

To extend the ministry of the radio program was a dream of Brenda Josee. She is a good friend and a great encouragement to me. Her beautiful and creative ideas have made this book a reality. She and Tammy Campbell compiled, organized, and edited the scripts, and Joette Whims and Lynn Copeland gave the material a final edit. Michelle Treiber coordinated the cover design and printing. I also thank my dear husband, Bill, my greatest source of inspiration and encouragement, with whom I have enjoyed the adventure of trusting God for over fifty years.

My heartfelt thanks go to:

The current and former staff of *Women Today*—Judy Clark, Sallie Clingman, Pam Davis, Cherry Fields, Tina Hood, Liz Lazarian, JoAnn Lynch Licht, Robin Maroudi, Patty McClung, Kathy MacLeod, Judy Nelson, Anna Patterson, Laura Staudt Sherwood, Pam Sloop, Mary Ann White, Carrie Wright; the script writers—Christy Brain, Lisa Brockman, Rebecca Cotton, Angie Bruckner Grella, Keva Harrison, Kirsten Jarrett, Roger Kemp, Cindy Kinkaid, Tracy Lambert, Christi Mansfield, Linda Wall, Kara Austin Williams, Ann Wright; "The Committee" in Orlando; The Lighthouse Report; Ambassador Advertising; Evelyn Gibson; and Jim Sanders.

All of this to say, this book has been a gift to me from the hard work of others. I now present it to you. My prayer is that these devotionals will be an encouragement to you and will help you in a greater way to entrust *your heart into His hands*.

My dear friends,

The decision is now in the hands of the jury." We understand these familiar words.

"I will take matters into my own hands." Again, we know exactly what that means. Because we take hold of things physically with our hands, our hands symbolize control of situations, emotions, and ideas.

How many times have you asked someone, "Can you handle that?" There is One who is able to perfectly handle every aspect of your life. If you have accepted the Lord Jesus Christ as your Savior, the best way to describe the security of not only this life on earth, but also the eternal destiny of your soul, is to picture *your heart in the hands of God!*

The God who promised the descendants of Abraham, "I will uphold you with my righteous right hand" (Isaiah 41:10) also holds your heart in His hands.

Life is often hectic, and the responsibilities of women in our culture place enormous demands on our physical and emotional energy. By the time we meet the needs of the day, we may find little time to seek God's heart and find solace in the strength of His hands.

I love to see a mother cradle the head of her crying newborn in her hands and gently stroke away the tears.

The security that infant feels with the familiar touch of his mother calms him to sleep. That's the scene I picture when I come to God in prayer for my own needs and express my frustrations to Him. Just sitting quietly before Him, I can sense His gentle touch caressing my aching heart, and my burden is soon lifted.

King David said it so perfectly: "You open your hand and satisfy the desires of every living thing" (Psalm 145:16).

If you have not placed your heart in His hands, please do so today. You may have accepted the Lord Jesus as your Savior but are still struggling in your life because you don't know the security, comfort, and guidance of His hand. The psalmist assures you:

He who dwells in the shelter of the Most High
will rest in the shadow of the Almighty.
I will say of the LORD, "He is my refuge and my fortress,
my God, in whom I trust." (Psalm 91:1,2)

Give Him your whole heart and experience the peace and joy that will follow you through every season of your life.

From my joyful heart to yours,

Vonette Z. Bright

Delighting in My Lord

*I delight greatly in the LORD; my soul
rejoices in my God.*

ISAIAH 61:10

The first scent of autumn in the air. For the many
years we lived in the San Bernardino Mountains, the
cooler temperatures were a welcome relief to the hot
summer nights and scorching days. We didn't have tree-
lined roadways with leaves creating curtains of color.
But we did have enough trees to require leaf raking.

My friend told me a story about two little boys who
taught her a profound lesson as she drove through her
neighborhood one autumn day. The rake was twice as
tall as the little boy was, and the pile of leaves was
stacked high above his head. The sense of accomplishment was visible in his expression. But just as he pulled
the last clump of leaves into the heap, a gust of wind

scattered most of them back onto the lawn. The look on the little boy's face changed from bewilderment to frustration, and he angrily dropped the rake, hopped on his bicycle, and rode down the street to join his friends at play.

On the next block, another boy was raking leaves, but each time he accumulated a small pile, he pushed them into a plastic bag, tied the top, and tossed it onto the sidewalk. The wind continued to blow, and the bags rolled around like oversized beach balls. But the leaves were contained, so his work was not in vain.

This story reinforces a spiritual truth. Just when we think we have it all together, the winds of adversity can displace everything we hold dear. Planning ahead for times of adversity may sound impossible, but spiritually it is not only possible but necessary.

The best way to prepare for unexpected "gusts" is to develop a relationship with Christ rooted so deeply in His Word that at any moment we can retreat to the security of His protective hand. Telling the Savior our anxious concerns allows us to bring our thoughts captive and let the Holy Spirit guide our reactions.

The Willing Heart

We must not be satisfied with exteriorly submitting to obedience and in things that are easy, but we must obey with whole heart and in things the most difficult. For the greater the difficulty, the greater also is the merit of obedience. Can we refuse to submit to man for God's sake when God, for love of us, submits to man, even to His very executioners?

Jesus Christ was willingly obedient during His whole life and even unto the death of the cross, and am I unwilling to spend my life in the exercise of obedience and to make it my cross and my merit?

THOMAS A KEMPIS
Imitation of Christ

I don't know if my husband originated the phrase, but we've stated it so many times that we feel ownership: "God is more interested in availability than ability."

Being available to God should come naturally to the woman who has placed her heart in His hands. Knowing that the hands holding our life securely will also guide our life safely gives us the confidence to take bold steps of faith and actively become a breath of fresh air to a world stifled by Satan.

I have seen young women timidly step out in faith and become available to serve. Many women around the world are making a positive impact on people and cultures simply because they made themselves available.

"Being available" doesn't mean we will be required to leave husband and home to accept some demanding task. Neither is it a passive attitude where we sit and wait for something to drop like autumn leaves into our lap. We need to seek opportunities to share our faith and demonstrate a biblical view of life.

As our willing heart actively pursues a deeper relationship with God, He will send opportunities beyond our imagination—but we must choose to accept them. When a heart directed by the Holy Spirit embraces with loving obedience the challenge at hand, great accomplishments for Christ are realized.

DAY 1

In 1985, Sara founded Orlando's House of Hope, a home for runaway teenage girls. It is a home where spiritual counseling and prayer were first priorities for the staff.

House of Hope

The House of Hope was established through a series of miracles—from raising the money to buying land, to hiring trained staff and volunteers. Once the doors of the house opened to the first residents, the miracles continued in the hearts and lives of troubled girls and their families.

The House of Hope provides twenty-five teenage girls —ages twelve to seventeen—with a Christ-centered refuge from a life of degradation and exploitation. The basic goals are to introduce each girl to Christ and to stimulate family reconciliation. This is done through education, Christian counseling, and spiritual guidance—administered in a loving, home-style environment. And, as one staff member emphatically added, a lot of prayer.

Sara told me that she saw more change in the lives of her girls in eight months than during her fifteen years in a government institution. She and her staff attribute the transformed lives to the life-changing work of Jesus Christ in the hearts of the girls and their families.

Sara explained the success of the program to me. At the time we spoke, more than 225 girls had gone through the program, and not one had graduated without asking Jesus Christ to come into her heart. Only two were lost back to the streets.

One woman. One dream. Hundreds of changed lives.

What about you? What's your dream? Have you ever considered that God could use you to make a difference right where you are? Is there a burden on your heart today, something you care deeply about—an issue or an area in life that you'd like to see changed?

God can use you. Together, one woman at a time, we can help to change the world.

HIS WORD
"Because of the service by which you have proved yourselves, men will praise God for the obedience that accompanies your confession of the gospel of Christ, and for your generosity in sharing with them and with everyone else" (2 Corinthians 9:13).

MY PART
It doesn't take an army to change the world. Changing the world always begins with one person. It starts with you and me. Take the initiative today to follow the dream God has given you for helping people. Pray for God's guidance, then map out a plan of action.

MY STUDY
1 Samuel 12:24;
Psalm 25:4–6

DAY 2

One day, Mary was watching TV and happened upon a special news commentary on Somalia. Depressed at the whole situation, she flipped to another channel.

Suddenly, she was rebuked about her reaction. She thought, *When God sees disaster, He doesn't turn the channel. He doesn't ignore the suffering in Somalia, and neither can I.*

So Mary flipped back to the channel, and there she saw something she'll never forget—the picture of an infant trying to nurse from the breast of his dead mother.

Mary recalled, "Suddenly, God had my attention. I began to weep for the mothers of Somalia. I imagined having to hunt for food and run in the streets to get it for my children."

Ten months later, she flew to Somalia herself and had the opportunity to share Christ with Muslim women there. Reaching out to women who didn't know about Jesus, she reveled in bringing Living Water to thirsty Somalians.

You know what I love about Mary? She responded

to that stirring in her heart and did something. God used her because she was willing to go and do whatever He asked of her.

In Matthew 10:8, Jesus says to His disciples and to us, "Freely you have received, freely give." God has given us so many blessings at absolutely no cost to us, so we must do the same for others. This may include a simple gesture like giving up your seat for someone on a crowded bus, or traveling around the world to feed hungry people.

Let's be inspired by Mary's example today. The next time opportunity knocks at your door, whether you're in your living room, at the office, in the supermarket, or somewhere else, don't turn the channel. Don't look away. Do something!

If you do, you will become rich in a way you've never experienced before.

HIS WORD
"Command them to do good, to be rich in good deeds, and to be generous and willing to share" (1 Timothy 6:18).

MY PART
"Loving Lord Jesus, please forgive me for turning away from the needy around me. Thank You for opening my eyes to the apathy I have had in my heart. I now commit myself to being more sensitive to Your leading and to helping others as I can. Amen."

MY STUDY
Deuteronomy 15:10,11; Proverbs 14:31

Robin was a single mother providing for herself and two small girls on her meager income. After paying for rent and child-care, she had a small amount left over for food.

Because Robin didn't have money for the deposit, she and her girls were without electricity. No electricity meant no hot water, no refrigerator, no stove, no lights, no heat!

Lifeline of Hope

They lived one day at a time. Robin would buy just enough food for a single day and keep it in a cooler. Food was cooked on a small charcoal grill. They used a kerosene lamp to provide light.

During that time, Robin said, "I just wanted to give up; I felt like there was no hope. As a mother, I felt like a failure because I couldn't even provide the basics for my kids!"

Embarrassed, Robin kept her plight to herself. She didn't want to tell her family or coworkers. No one seemed to notice Robin's predicament.

But one astute, caring neighbor did! As Michelle made her way up the stairs to her own place each night, she noticed that there were no lights coming from Robin's apartment.

One day, Michelle and Robin bumped into each other and began to chat. Robin told her the whole story.

Michelle's resources were limited so she couldn't do much, but she could do something. She ran an extension cord from her apartment, over the balcony, into Robin's apartment. Now Robin and the girls could turn on a light or listen to the radio—things you and I take for granted.

Something like running an extension cord might seem quite trivial—even primitive. But in this time of great need, it was a lifeline of hope.

Dear friend, one small act could give the encouragement and hope someone needs to face another day. And it can also open the door to further ministry in that person's life.

HIS WORD
"Let no debt remain outstanding, except the continuing debt to love one another, for he who loves his fellowman has fulfilled the law" (Romans 13:8).

MY PART
I encourage you to be a student of those around you. Get to know your neighbors and your coworkers. Notice things about them. Ask questions. And when you learn of a need, think creatively about at least one thing you can do to help.

MY STUDY
Psalm 147:10,11; Lamentations 3:19–24

DAY 4

Kim couldn't bear the thought of revealing her secret struggle. She was wasting away inside with guilt about her compulsion.

Free From Bondage

Finally, she cried out to a friend, "I throw up my food!" She then described the classic patterns of anorexia and bulimia—obsessing with food and exercise, and eating, then purging. Even a glance at a vending machine would ignite her lust for food and trigger a binge.

Today, Kim is helping young people overcome this devastating compulsion, an epidemic among high school and college women. It's likely you know people who are trapped in the jaws of some compulsive disorder. How can you encourage and strengthen them?

Let me share several principles Kim passed along:

- First, be a non-threatening, gracious friend. You can't make people admit they need help (their first step toward healing), but you can be available to them.
- Be a source of acceptance as well as accountability.

Lovingly listen and be supportive, but ask the tough questions when needed.

- Get into the Word with them. Consistent Bible reading was the key to Kim's recovery. God's Word became her food as she memorized Scripture. She was able to replace wrong, compulsive thinking with His righteous truth.
- Pray for them fervently!
- Most of us are not certified counselors. Recognize when your friends need more help than you are able to give, and refer them to someone who can help.

Jesus said, "Then you will know the truth, and the truth will set you free" (John 8:32). His truth set Kim free from the bondage of a compulsive eating disorder.

Be a willing model and messenger of truth, bringing freedom and hope to the captives around you.

HIS WORD
"Therefore each of you must put off falsehood and speak truthfully to his neighbor, for we are all members of one body" (Ephesians 4:25).

MY PART
Do you know someone struggling with a compulsive disorder? Ask God to give you wisdom and courage to help your friend. Perhaps you can also discretely ask others to pray for this person as well. You can make a difference in someone's life.

MY STUDY
Psalm 20:1,2; Isaiah 58:9,10

DAY 5

Daniel is one of my heroes. As a teenager held captive in Babylon, he was selected by the king's officials for a royal education. He quickly rose to become one of the king's most influential advisors and friends.

Like Daniel

A student in the king's court, Daniel had access to all the luxuries of the palace—sumptuous food, rare wine, and scintillating discussions with the country's intellectual leaders.

Daniel took advantage of the great education. *But he refused to indulge in the king's food and wine*. Why? The food and wine were dedicated to the Babylonian gods before they were served, and Daniel didn't want to compromise his worship of the one true God.

He refused to turn away from his convictions, even if it meant offending the king. Daniel could have been killed for his refusal, but he dared to face that consequence.

God honored Daniel for his integrity, giving him exceptional knowledge and understanding. After three years, the king tested Daniel and the other young men to see who was best and brightest. Guess who won the contest! Daniel.

Daniel served the king for at least seventy years. Many times he reiterated his commitment to live by the Word of God regardless of the consequences.

But this life of faith might never have been possible if Daniel hadn't lived out his convictions at the first opportunity. By taking a public stand for God in the beginning, he laid a solid foundation for a life of consistent faith.

Daniel decided to please God regardless of the consequences. He declined to do anything displeasing to the Lord, and God blessed Daniel with great spiritual growth.

God wants your devotion and mine as well. Whether you're rearing children at home or working in the marketplace, integrity marks the life truly committed to God.

Dare to be a Daniel. God will bless you.

HIS WORD

"The LORD has dealt with me according to my righteousness; according to the cleanness of my hands He has rewarded me"
(Psalm 18:20).

MY PART

How committed are you to God as the Lord of your life? Do you stand up for God and His truth? Refresh your commitment to God and His principles. Then ask Him for the courage you need to live them daily.

MY STUDY

2 Samuel 22:21,22; Ephesians 6:5–8

Have you ever watched two preschoolers fight over a toy? Neither is willing to share, so they both end up miserable!

A Cheerful Giver

My friends Lin and Byron developed some creative and successful ways to teach their children to give cheerfully to others. They understand young children need to *see* the results of their gifts if they're to understand the joy of giving and sharing.

The Smith family began by adopting a needy family at Christmas time. Each year, the Smith children set aside part of their Christmas gift money to buy presents for the children of that family. It became a joyous annual tradition.

Their tradition led the family to make cheerful giving a daily occurrence. One evening, the family saw a World Vision special on television. The Smith children were touched when they saw youngsters their own age going hungry.

Together, the family decided to do something very creative. After much discussion, they planned to eat a refugee-type meal once a week. It would consist of a little rice or oatmeal. The money they saved by eating less they would send to World Vision for famine relief in Africa.

That weekly lesson taught the whole family to appreciate the abundance of food they usually took for granted.

My friend, it is very exciting to watch your children develop compassion for others and a willingness to share with those in need. You need to take the first step by setting an example.

As you model generosity and sacrificial giving, explain to your children why you're motivated to share. Teach them that when we give to those in need, we are obeying Jesus, who was very serious about the importance of giving.

Finally, explain that the reward of passing on our blessings is great. God has promised an eternal reward in heaven. But He has also promised the greatest earthly reward we could want—joy.

HIS WORD
"Give, and it will be given to you. A good measure, pressed down, shaken together and running over, will be poured into your lap. For with the measure you use, it will be measured to you" (Luke 6:38).

MY PART
If you receive unexpected money, consider donating it to a friend in need. Make a practice of inviting people to your home for dinner after church. Open your home to your children's friends; let them know your home is a safe place to be. Delight in sharing the Lord's blessings.

MY STUDY
Deuteronomy 24:19–22; Psalm 112:9

A woman was riding her bike along her favorite mountain trail, which she traversed every morning. The river sparkled beside her, the sun was shining brightly, and the warmth of the breeze felt good to her shoulders.

Jump In

Then she heard screams coming from below. "Help me," someone said. "You've got to help me!"

Without hesitation, she jumped off her bike and slid down the embankment nearly a hundred yards to the river. She hopped into the water and waded out where she could put her arms underneath the drowning woman.

The current was stronger than she'd anticipated, and suddenly they were both moving rapidly downstream. She realized they were in trouble and began to call out for help.

As they came around a bend, they saw three people perched on a ledge, watching. Two of them were videotaping their plight!

She screamed, "Can't you see we're drowning? Shut the cameras off, jump in the water, and help us!"

The spectators dropped their cameras and ran downriver. The three of them waded out into the current and created a human chain. When the two desperate women arrived, they were able to use their collective strength to catch them and pull them safely to the shore.

What can we learn from this story?

Friend, we're watching the very nation we love begin to sink. We're in trouble. We have a moral dilemma of historic proportions on our hands. Sometimes it feels like we have spectators on the shore who are doing nothing more than documenting the tragedy on video!

What kind of contribution can you make?

Working together, we can make a difference, shaping a nation for future generations to enjoy and giving glory to God. God bless you as you look for ways to serve Him. You'll be glad you did.

HIS WORD
"Blessed is the nation whose God is the LORD, *the people He chose for His inheritance" (Psalm 33:12).*

MY PART
Perhaps you see a need in your local school, or you're outraged by the anti-God politics in your community. Maybe you're concerned about the sanctity of human life, and you have yet to help your local crisis pregnancy center. Make a commitment to give more time and energy to these worthy causes. You will make a difference.

MY STUDY
Isaiah 60:10–12; Titus 3:1,2

DAY 8

During Adolf Hitler's reign of terror in World War II, there were glimpses of goodness and heroism in those who opposed him.

At the beginning of the war, twenty Nazi soldiers arrived in a village with two empty buses. They were there to take away the Jews who were in hiding.

True Heroism

The soldiers confronted one of the local pastors. At the risk of his life and the lives of his parishioners, the pastor quietly, but defiantly, refused to hand over a single Jew who had come to him for refuge.

Incredibly, the Nazis went away. But as the war dragged on, they came back again and again, searching for Jews.

Several villagers were arrested; some were killed. However, not a single one of their endangered Jewish friends was betrayed during the entire occupation. In fact, during those four years, the villagers actively rescued as many as 3,000 Jews—many of them children.

Here, in the midst of human cruelty and depravity of the *worst* kind, we find a story of heroism of the *best* kind.

I live in Orlando, Florida, and if I live here the rest of my life, I'll probably never have the opportunity to rescue 3,000 people from death. So what does it mean to be a hero in my world and yours?

All it requires is honoring God in the little things, as well as the big. That's it. It's simply being a woman of conviction. A woman who is willing to step out and speak for what is right, to become an activist rather than a spectator, to risk ridicule or embarrassment.

Is this easy? Certainly not! But that's why it's heroic.

Decide today that you're willing to be a hero. Like the citizens of that tiny village, it means doing what is right—not simply what is easy.

Dear friend, true heroism is an ordinary life lived well.

HIS WORD
"Whatever you do, work at it with all your heart, as working for the Lord, not for men" (Colossians 3:23).

MY PART
Pray this wonderful prayer offered by the French philosopher Pascal: "Lord, help me do great things as though they were little, since I do them with Your powers; and help me to do little things as though they were great, because I do them in Your name."

MY STUDY
Esther 4:12–16; Psalm 84:10,11

DAY 9

Shannon was a senior in high school. When she came home one evening, her mother told her about a school-board meeting that night. Student-led prayer at the graduation ceremony could get voted down.

Take a Stand

Without hesitation, Shannon left for the meeting. She had no idea what she'd say to the school board. She could only think, *If I don't take a stand, who will?*

Shannon felt that Jesus was her best Friend, and true friends always stand up for each other. She wanted to end her twelve long years of school by thanking God in prayer.

That night, as Shannon spoke to the board members, she was nervous—but impassioned about what she knew was right.

As the meeting came to an end, it was time to vote. With one vote remaining, the count was a tie. The last board member said, "This young lady has really influenced me." Then he cast his vote in favor of prayer.

Shannon was relieved but unprepared for the flood of media attention that followed. During the late local news that night, a video clip of Shannon was telecast, showing her standing before the school board.

Unfortunately, the next day, a motion was filed to stop the school board's decision. A non-profit organization came to Shannon's legal aid. A temporary court injunction upheld the school-board decision, so the senior class representative prayed at the graduation ceremony.

Can one person really make a difference? Shannon did. Her act of courage made a huge difference.

My prayer is that each of us will be ready to stand up and be involved as representatives of the living God.

Shannon's story gives me courage. I hope it does you, too. Today's high school students are tomorrow's national leaders. By influencing their lives for Christ in this generation, we can expect to have more *good news* in the next!

HIS WORD

"With your help I can advance against a troop; with my God I can scale a wall" (Psalm 18:29).

MY PART

Whether you're a student, a parent, a teacher, or just a concerned citizen, you can scale a wall wherever you are. You can join a prayer group, write a letter, attend a school-board meeting, or teach a Bible study. One stone thrown in a pond can ripple across the whole body of water.

MY STUDY

Micah 3:8; Hebrews 11:30

Charles Finney was one of the greatest preachers of all time. Thousands came to Christ as a result of his ministry.

But most of us have never heard the name of Lydia Andrews, the faithful woman who undergirded his ministry with prayer.

On Your Knees

Lydia began praying for Charles long before he became a Christian. Finney, a lawyer by profession, was cynical about the church, but Lydia prayed for his salvation.

Several years after his conversion, they married. She continued to support his ministry with prayer. In fact, prayer was the hallmark of Finney's outreach. Lydia organized ten prayer groups who met every day in Rochester, New York, solely to pray for the hand of God in Finney's preaching ministry.

These prayer meetings were huge! Crowds of up to a thousand people would gather to pray. Those who couldn't get into the packed church building would kneel in the snow outside! It was a marvelous movement of prayer in the 1800s.

The result? Countless thousands came to know Christ, and generations have been impacted by the ministry of Charles Finney.

I fear, at times, that Christians appeal to prayer as a last resort, hoping to change God's mind at the last minute. But when you pray, you are not choosing the last resort! You are choosing the *only* resort, what should be the *first* resort!

My friend, I urge you to pray. Pray for big things: that God will reach nations with His Word, that walls would fall, and that truth will prevail. But as you pray for the nations, never fail to pray for individuals, for the hearts of men and women who need the Savior.

Wherever you are in developing your prayer life, I want to challenge you to take the next step *on your knees*. You may never be a great preacher like Charles Finney, but you can be a great pray-er like Lydia Andrews.

HIS WORD
"They all joined together constantly in prayer, along with the women and Mary the mother of Jesus, and with his brothers" (Acts 1:14).

MY PART
"Holy Lord Jesus, thank You for the wonderful privilege of prayer. Forgive me for not making it the first resort whenever needs arise. I commit now to making prayer a vital part of my life and walk with You. In Your blessed name, amen."

MY STUDY
Psalm 122:6–9; Daniel 6:10–23

In his book *Fearfully and Wonderfully Made*, Dr. Paul Brand tells this story.

During the war, a cathedral in England was all but destroyed in a bombing raid. Following the war, German students rebuilt the bombed-out cathedral.

My Hands, His Heart

Work progressed on the building, but there was a large broken statue of Jesus. He was standing with arms outstretched, and on the statue were His words, "Come unto Me."

The German volunteers discussed at great length how the statue of Jesus could be restored. Careful patching could fix most of the statue, but Jesus' outstretched hands posed a much greater problem. Bomb fragments had destroyed them. Reshaping the hands would be a very delicate, tedious task. The workers decided it would be best to leave them as they were.

Today, this statue of Jesus has no hands, but the workers left another inscription: "Christ has no hands but ours."

Amazing! Out of destruction, God can raise up beautiful lessons of life!

Jesus dwelt among us for a short time. He had hands, and He used them—first as a carpenter and then as the loving Son of God. He embraced the leper, healed the lame, and tenderly held the children.

When He asked us to follow Him, He commissioned us to be His hands and carry on His ministry.

He told us to go and make disciples, to love our neighbors, to pray for one another, to feed His sheep. There are hundreds of other things. There are multitudes of ways you can be His hands and show His love.

Friend, find one thing you can do today to show the outstretched hands of Jesus and to reach out in His love. Watch how He confirms the work of *your* hands.

Remember, He has no hands but ours.

HIS WORD

"She opens her arms to the poor and extends her hands to the needy" (Proverbs 31:20).

MY PART

Call a friend, perhaps one you don't see often. Tell her you want to pray especially for her this week. Ask about her special needs, and do what you can to help. Pray for her every day the rest of the week, then follow up to see how God has answered.

MY STUDY

Leviticus 25:35; James 2:15–17

When Jan was in sixth grade, she asked her mom, Tara, to lead a Bible study for her class.

Tara was reluctant because she didn't feel qualified to teach children. But she told Jan she'd pray about it. Soon, she found herself writing out invitations.

The Children

The first week, six of Jan's classmates came, and they came week after week. Every Wednesday afternoon, those children came to hear Tara share about God. She prepared a snack, a Bible story, and a simple activity.

The children learned about God creating the world, about Adam and Eve, about Noah and all the animals. They learned about Jesus, that He was the Son of God, that He gave His very life to pay the penalty for man's sin, and that God, in His magnificent power, raised Jesus from the dead.

At the end of the school year, Tara planned to break for the summer. But the first Wednesday afternoon of the summer, her little Bible study group arrived on her front porch. The children had voted and decided they wanted to meet through the summer.

So Tara made popcorn and popped in the *JESUS* video. Based solely on the Gospel of Luke, this movie clearly tells the story of Jesus' life.

For the next few weeks, Tara showed the children segments of the film. Then she'd lead a discussion about what they'd seen. By the end of summer, each one of those children had placed their trust in Jesus.

There are so many children who don't have anyone to teach them about God. They'd love to be in a Bible study like Tara's. You may not feel qualified to lead one, but if God has put it on your heart, you *can* do it!

Dear friend, teach the children about God's love. Some day they will thank you. And they'll spend an eternity with Jesus!

HIS WORD
"Jesus called the children to Him and said, 'Let the little children come to me, and do not hinder them, for the kingdom of God belongs to such as these'" (Luke 18:16).

MY PART
Talk with your pastor or check with your local Christian bookstore for materials designed for children. Think of neighborhood children, your child's classmates, or fellow team members from soccer or softball. Invite several of those young people to your home for a Bible study. Your influence will be immeasurable and eternal.

MY STUDY
Proverbs 22:6; Isaiah 48:17

DAY 13

As a young woman, Becky Tirabassi committed herself to pray for at least one hour every day. Through the years, she's kept her commitment.

Becky is a well-known author and conference speaker. She tells this story in her book, *Wild Things Happen When I Pray*.

When You Pray

When Becky and her husband moved into a new neighborhood, she learned her neighbors' names right away. She wrote them in her prayer journal and prayed for each one every day. She prayed they'd learn of God's love and then trust Jesus Christ.

But Becky wasn't putting action to her prayers. She wasn't looking for opportunities to share the gospel message. In fact, she actually thought God would hear her prayers and then lead her neighbors to *other* Christians in their lives. And then *they'd* invite them to church and share their faith with them.

After more than three years of praying for her neighbors, name by name, something happened. One day, Becky was driving home from teaching an aerobics class. As was her habit, she was listening to Pastor Charles Stanley's radio program, *In Touch*.

One sentence in Dr. Stanley's message pierced Becky's heart. He said, "Don't pray about anything you wouldn't want God to do through you." Becky began to realize she just might be the very one God would want to use in the lives of her neighbors.

When Becky's neighbor Barbara knocked on the door a few days later, Becky began putting action to her prayers. First, she told Barbara how she prayed for her daily. Then, she invited her to church. As they became more acquainted, they talked often about church, God, and faith. Eventually, Barbara placed her faith in Christ.

Oh, dear friend, your neighbors need you to pray for them *and* tell them about God's love and forgiveness. Allow God to use you to tell others of His love. As you do, you'll develop friendships that will last through eternity.

HIS WORD
"The LORD detests the sacrifice of the wicked, but the prayer of the upright pleases him" (Proverbs 15:8).

MY PART
Pray faithfully, name by name, for your neighbors, and ask God to give you opportunities to share your faith. Invite your next-door neighbor over for coffee. Have a barbecue for the family across the street. Take a crafts class with the woman down the block. Most importantly, take the time to share your faith in Christ and lead them to His love and grace.

MY STUDY
Job 42:10;
Jude 20–23

Jay loves fishing. When he landed one of the biggest fish in a contest, he was awarded a nice cash prize.

Jay considered the prize money a gift from God, so he wanted to use it wisely. He wondered whether he should save it, invest it, or spend it on family needs.

Secret Angel

In the meantime, Jay's eight-year-old daughter, Brittany, expressed concern about a classmate. Brittany's friend Cassie was often teased by other children. Cassie wore old clothes and rarely smiled. Brittany wanted to help her friend, so she asked her dad if they could use some of his prize money to help Cassie.

He loved the idea and was delighted at his young daughter's desire to help someone. So Brittany and her mother, Rita, bought clothes, shoes, and toys for Cassie.

To remain anonymous, they asked a teacher to deliver their surprise. When Brittany next saw her, Cassie said with delight that a "secret angel" had sent the gifts. Brittany was thrilled. She said, "Mom, I didn't know Cassie could smile like that!"

Because Rita knew a small gift was just a bandage

for Cassie's problem, she had included a note to Cassie's mom in Cassie's gift box. She told her that as Christians they'd like to help her. The two women developed a friendship, and Rita was able to share the gospel message of God's love with Cassie's mom. Rita, Jay, and Brittany continue to help with the family's needs.

Oh, dear friend, there are people right next door, down the street, or in the adjacent office who need your help. They need someone to reach out and care, someone to be a friend.

God wants us to show His love to others in tangible ways. Have a willing heart to help. And remember, whatever you do, always take time to share God's message of love. Like Cassie, you'll be God's secret angel!

HIS WORD
"If anyone has material possessions and sees his brother in need but has no pity on him, how can the love of God be in him? Dear children, let us not love with words or tongue but with actions and in truth" (1 John 3:17,18).

MY PART
"Merciful God, please forgive me for not sharing out of the abundance of Your blessings. Because You have commanded us to love one another, I want to show my love in tangible ways. Help me to be sensitive to the needs of others and to have a giving spirit. Amen."

MY STUDY
Proverbs 22:2; Isaiah 61:1–3

DAY 15

First Corinthians 13:1 says, "If I speak in the tongues of men and of angels, but have not love, I am only a resounding gong or a clanging cymbal." Love, *real* love, is not just words. *God's* love is action!

Love in Action

Is your home a place where friends, neighbors, and visitors feel welcome? Or is your home a refuge for only you?

When it comes to expressing God's love, do you do more than talk about it? Do you demonstrate your love?

Chris and Karen demonstrate God's love through hospitality. They've helped many of us understand some of the practical ways of using our homes. They remind us that the amount of love in a home is far more important than the amount of space.

A ministry of hospitality can begin by inviting people over to dinner—international students, senior adults, new church members, neighbors, single moms, visiting missionaries.

Let me challenge you. Within the next month, invite someone to your home who's never been there. Ask

God to show you who that would be—a neighbor, a coworker, the family of your child's friend. Ask God to give you an idea of what to do for the evening.

Ask God to make the time meaningful and what He wants it to be. Remember, as a Christian you are God's ambassador; you represent Him. Our goal should be to minister to people, not just to entertain.

Author Karen Mains wrote, "True hospitality comes before pride. It has nothing to do with impressing people, but everything to do with making them feel welcome and wanted."

We have a great opportunity to help others know and experience the love of Jesus for themselves. Invite them in! With each visitor comes a chance to touch that person for eternity, to love that person, and to point him or her to the Lord.

HIS WORD
"In the same way, faith by itself, if it is not accompanied by action, is dead" (James 2:17).

MY PART
"Loving Lord Jesus, as You gave Your life willingly and freely, so I want to give of myself to others. I commit myself and my home to You. Help me to use them for Your glory. Amen."

MY STUDY
Joshua 24:15; Proverbs 11:24

DAY 16

The Bible says, "In his heart a man plans his course, but the LORD determines his steps" (Proverbs 16:9).

That's what Emma Morris found out a few years ago. The corporation she worked for offered her a promotion, but the new position would require traveling and time away from her husband.

Your Mission Field

"At the same time," she said, "I felt a strong call to go into full-time ministry."

To make a wise and informed choice, Emma sought guidance through prayer and God's Word. Then she spoke to her husband and several dear friends. She examined her gifts and talents and how they might be used in a ministry. As she carefully considered all her options, the tug on her heart to go into ministry only increased. So she turned down the promotion and left the company.

While investigating ministry opportunities, she began working as a consultant. Her meetings took her into the offices of CEOs of various companies. What happened surprised her. She said, "In every case, I was able to share my faith with the person who most influenced the rest of the organization."

Months later, she realized she was, indeed, a full-time missionary. She said, "My mission field was the business world and, specifically, its leaders!"

Emma knew in her heart that she needed to reach out to others with God's love. As she did, God showed her that her mission field was right where she was.

Friend, if you're not sharing God's love in your neighborhood and community, you won't do it in the mission field either. The best training ground in the world for evangelism is right where you are.

Begin talking about Jesus Christ wherever you go because, at this moment, that's your mission field.

HIS WORD

"We proclaim him, admonishing and teaching everyone with all wisdom, so that we may present everyone perfect in Christ. To this end I labor, struggling with all his energy, which so powerfully works in me" (Colossians 1:28,29).

MY PART

Friend, you can make a difference for Christ right where you are. There are people who need a Savior just outside your front door, down the street, and in your workplace. Ask God for boldness as you seek to share His life-giving Gift with others.

MY STUDY

Psalm 28:8,9; Habakkuk 3:2

DAY 17

After graduating from college in Boston, Julie and a roommate moved to New York City to pursue careers in journalism. Unfortunately, the competition was overwhelming, so Julie was forced to take a temporary job as a waitress.

His Passion

It didn't take long for Julie to feel disillusioned. Getting a job was tougher than she thought. While waitressing, Julie saw the seedy side of New York and began to wonder if she'd ever have a legitimate career.

Finally, she got an interview for a page position at NBC.

About that time, Julie's sister, who lived in Miami, trusted Christ. As a result, she urged Julie to attend a worship service in New York.

It was at church that Julie met a woman who worked for ABC. When she told this seasoned professional about her upcoming interview, she told Julie she'd pray for her. Julie was impressed!

The interview was grueling. Several network directors and seven other applicants sat around a table as each candidate was grilled. It was a tough experience, but Julie got the position.

She was convinced prayer was the primary reason for success, so Julie took the woman who had prayed for her to lunch. The woman, in turn, invited her to a Bible study.

To Julie's surprise, at the Bible study she found authentic people who really wanted to know God—women who were not afraid to share their struggles and fears, fulfilled women who had purpose in their lives.

Through this group of women, Julie became a believer. She also began working in full-time ministry to reach professional women. Her passion for reaching women has exceeded her passion for journalism.

God has a way of turning His passion into your passion. If you will only follow Him wherever He leads, He will give you the desires of your heart. A heart devoted to Him will be blessed indeed.

HIS WORD
"In your unfailing love you will lead the people you have redeemed. In your strength you will guide them to your holy dwelling"
(Exodus 15:13).

MY PART
Make it your goal this week to reach out to a person like Julie. Go out for coffee. Talk to her about the direction of her life. Show your concern and interest. Then, commit yourself to pray for her. Become a friend. In a loving way, teach her what God has taught you in your own life.

MY STUDY
Psalm 5:11,12; John 10:3,4

DAY 18

As a missionary to Brazil, Karen helped to found the House of Hope, a Southern Baptist hospice to AIDS patients—prostitutes, homosexuals, and young mothers who've contracted AIDS.

"What a Pretty Girl!"

Karen prays with the patients. Her ten-year-old daughter, Katie, visits with patients as well. One day, Katie's attention was drawn to a young Brazilian mother whose once healthy body was now emaciated.

Katie's innocence allowed her to see beyond the sickness to the woman's clear, green eyes, framed by long dark lashes to a face that maintained striking beauty. "Look, Mommy," Katie called out, "what a pretty girl!"

That's when Karen realized how far she was from her quiet Alabama hometown. All because one day, her pastor encouraged the congregation to love and comfort the sick and dying, despite their spiritual condition. Right then and there, she unmistakably felt God telling her to go.

For so long, she'd pointed a finger of judgment at

those with AIDS. Today, she shares God's love. She said, "I was born and reared and lived my life in a comfort zone. Stepping out of that has been a real learning and growing experience."

Dear friend, you don't have to go to Brazil to help others and show God's love. But have you been willing to step out of your comfort zone? To reach beyond those borders to touch someone with the love of Jesus? Can you reach out in love and acceptance instead of pointing a finger of guilt and shame?

Jesus taught that we need to forgive one another and help each other recover from a sinful lifestyle. There are hurting people right outside your front door. They need someone like you to encourage them with God's message of love. Reach out to them today.

Step out of your comfort zone so that you too can look beyond appearances and say, "Look! What a pretty girl!"

HIS WORD

"When he saw the crowds, he had compassion on them, because they were harassed and helpless, like sheep without a shepherd. Then he said to his disciples, 'The harvest is plentiful but the workers are few. Ask the Lord of the harvest, therefore, to send out workers into his harvest field'" (Matthew 9:36–38).

MY PART

"Lord Jesus, forgive me for pointing fingers of blame instead of reaching out in love. I want to follow Your example of forgiveness and love, to give hope to those who have none. In Your name, amen."

MY STUDY

1 Chronicles 28:9,10; Psalm 51:12

DAY 19

It was a dark day when Ann's neighbor discovered that she'd been abandoned by her husband. They'd been married forty-two years. Ann's neighbor was a Christian, and the breakup of her marriage was devastating.

Love Your Neighbor

Ann began to reach out to her neighbor, and a deep friendship grew. They studied the Bible together, memorized Scripture, and sought God's direction. Ann stepped right in and became an encouragement to her new friend. Before long, God's love began to take over, creating something very beautiful out of a broken life.

To the right and left of your home, up and down the street, are households filled with opportunities for ministry. In many of those homes, men and women are enduring tremendous personal pain and suffering, much of it completely unnoticed by those nearby.

Do you know the names of those who live in your apartment complex or your neighborhood? Do you have any idea what they're going through—good or bad?

Today, Ann's neighbor is in ministry overseas. She trusted God, by faith, to open this door of opportunity, which He did. She's in Ecuador, using her skills to help spread the gospel in South America.

My friend, be looking for those opportunities to reach out to women in need, women who live next door or down the street. As we reach out right where we live, we will eventually reach the world.

It's easier than you think. Jesus put it very simply in Matthew 5:43: "Love your neighbor."

Here's what I think He meant: Do for others what you'd want someone to do for you. If you were in need, what would you appreciate? How would you want someone to respond when you face a crisis? What would you want her to say and do for you? Then love your neighbor with the love of Jesus, and find a way to show that love.

HIS WORD
"Do not forsake your friend and the friend of your father, and do not go to your brother's house when disaster strikes you—better a neighbor nearby than a brother far away" (Proverbs 27:10).

MY PART
How well do you know your neighbors? You can get to know them by planning opportunities to socialize, such as block parties, barbecues, and dinners. Take the initiative and help to organize the events. That is the first step in being able to share God's love with them.

MY STUDY
Leviticus 25:35; Romans 13:9,10

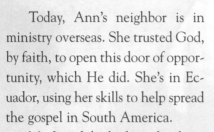

THE WILLING HEART

DAY 20

I t was a cold, wintry day. Sleet pelted the streets, making it a slushy walk to New York's Grand Central Station. People walked briskly with their heads huddled inside their coat collars, hardly noticing one another in their fight against the weather.

Simple Kindness

One young man struggled with two large, heavy suitcases. Slipping and sliding, he rushed to catch a train. Suddenly, another man reached out his hand and grabbed one of the suitcases. In a pleasant voice, he said, "Let me have that, Brother. In this bad weather, it's hard to carry so much!"

At first, the young man was apprehensive about the man's help. But as he looked up, the friendly smile put him at ease. As they walked together, they struck up a conversation like two long-lost friends.

Several years later, the young man, the great educator Booker T. Washington, said, "That kindly deed was my introduction to Theodore Roosevelt."

Friend, reach out to help someone with a heavy load. A simple act of kindness could be the key to winning someone's heart to faith in Christ.

God tells us several times in Scripture to be kind to each other:

- "Therefore, as God's chosen people, holy and dearly loved, clothe yourselves with compassion, kindness, humility, gentleness and patience" (Colossians 3:12).
- "Be kind and compassionate to one another" (Ephesians 4:32).
- "The Lord's servant...must be kind to everyone" (2 Timothy 2:24).

Kindness is attractive. People appreciate kindness. The grocery store clerk needs a smile and a courteous "thank you." The taxi driver dodging traffic for hours could use a bigger-than-usual tip. The faithful babysitter would enjoy a movie ticket for herself and a friend.

I'm sure you can think of many more acts of kindness. By demonstrating kindness, you are obeying God's command and showing His love to others.

HIS WORD
"Finally, all of you, live in harmony with one another; be sympathetic, love as brothers, be compassionate and humble" (1 Peter 3:8).

MY PART
Today, make a list of at least five specific acts of kindness that you can do in the next week to show God's love to those you encounter each day. After you complete each action listed, note the person's response and your own feelings about the interaction.

MY STUDY
Ruth 2:20; Proverbs 14:21

Jonathan was a lonely little boy who seemed to have a knack for getting into trouble. One day while playing with matches, he started the grass on fire in the yard of an elderly woman who lived next door to Norma Jean.

A Lifetime of Influence

"He's no good," the elderly neighbor complained to Norma Jean. "He'll never amount to anything. I don't understand why you even waste your time with him." After the fire, Norma Jean wondered, too.

But Norma Jean, the mother of two toddlers, cared for this little child who hungered for love and attention. He'd come to her home for cookies and to play with her children. She'd tell him stories about Jesus. Sometimes, Jonathan would go to church with her family.

Unfortunately, Norma Jean was pressured by the elderly neighbor not to invite Jonathan over anymore. After that, Jonathan's mom, a working single mother, wanted him to stop going to church with them. Norma Jean's opportunity for influencing this child diminished.

Norma Jean's family eventually moved away. Whenever Jonathan popped into her mind, she prayed for him.

Several years later, as she put her son on a bus to a Christian youth event, a voice called out, "Hey, I know you." It was Jonathan.

Norma Jean was anxious to know if he'd placed his trust in Christ. She was thrilled to hear his answer. "Yes!" he said. "I was saved two years ago." Their conversation was brief. But as Jonathan turned to leave, he called back to Norma Jean, "Thanks for all the cookies."

A busy young woman took time to be a friend to a lonely little boy, and God used her influence to help lead him to faith.

Ask God to show you the child who needs love and attention. Open your heart to him or her. Your influence will last a lifetime. One day you'll hear, "Thanks for all the cookies." It will melt your heart!

HIS WORD
"May the Lord make your love increase and overflow for each other and for everyone else, just as ours does for you" (1 Thessalonians 3:12).

MY PART
"Lord Jesus, You love the little children. Please help me to love them as You do. I desire to be sensitive to their needs and hurts so I can let Your love show through me. In Your wonderful name, amen."

MY STUDY
Psalm 78:5–8; Isaiah 40:11

DAY 22

Nancy Wilson has been a Crusade staff member for many years. Although she's small, she's a fireball of energy with a contagious love for God. She easily shares God's message of love and forgiveness wherever she goes.

Contagious Faith

Once, Nancy and I were both at a conference with leaders in our ministry. It was a typical conference with many meetings, and we had a few very informal buffet-style meals in a large conference room.

During those mealtimes, lots of conversations were going on among the ministry leaders. The waiters and waitresses mingled quietly and courteously among us. No one really noticed them. Except Nancy.

She noticed Earl. Earl was standing back, keeping an eye out for empty plates and glasses. So with her big, warm smile, Nancy approached Earl. She began talking with him.

Nancy carries little "blessing cards." As she pulled one out, she said, "Earl, I want to give you a blessing today." Then she handed him the card, which told of God's great love.

As he looked at the card, Nancy asked, "Earl, do you know God's love?" Earl read the card, but he didn't directly answer Nancy's question. He said, "I'll give it to my wife."

In Nancy's sweet way, she said, "No, Earl, God told me to give it to *you!*"

Then they began to talk about God. Nancy shared the gospel message with Earl. Right there, in the hustle and bustle of lunch, Earl trusted Jesus Christ as his Savior and Lord.

That's "lifestyle evangelism." It's simply talking with those in our midst about God's great love.

Take note of five people you see every week whom no one really notices. Pray for those on your list to be open to God's love. Ask Him for opportunities to share your faith.

Delight in telling others about God's love wherever you go. Like Nancy, your love for God will become contagious.

HIS WORD
"'Everyone who calls on the name of the Lord will be saved.' How, then, can they call on the one they have not believed in? And how can they believe in the one of whom they have not heard? And how can they hear without someone preaching to them?" (Romans 10:13,14).

MY PART
"Wonderful Lord Jesus, I confess that I have not taken advantage of opportunities to share Your love and forgiveness. I want to be prepared to tell others about You and to take the initiative in opportunities I encounter. In Your holy name, amen."

MY STUDY
Psalm 105:1; Joel 2:32

DAY 23

The annual National Day of Prayer (the first Thursday of May) was approaching. This day has been set aside for people of America to pray for leaders of our nation, our communities, our homes, and each other.

Not in Vain

Wendi looked forward to this day with great anticipation. She hoped one of her coworkers would arrange a prayer time. Nobody did. Finally, Wendi determined that maybe she should be the person to organize this meaningful time. So with faith that her labor would not be in vain, Wendi posted on the employee time clock a sign that read: "Today is the National Day of Prayer. If you're interested in praying for our country, contact Wendi."

Then she waited for people to respond. No one contacted her, but when she called some of her coworkers with a personal invitation, five joined her to pray. The time was meaningful, but what really made an impression on Wendi was what happened afterward. One of Wendi's coworkers asked Wendi to pray for her father.

Wendi didn't realize that a day of prayer for the nation would lead to her praying for a personal need of which she was previously unaware. Wendi said, "Now I'm more sensitive to others' needs. I'm consistently given the burden to pray for people. The Lord used my small, uncertain leap of faith to open doors to minister through prayer."

The apostle Paul wrote, "Therefore, my dear brothers, stand firm. Let nothing move you. Always give yourselves fully to the work of the Lord, because you know that your labor in the Lord is not in vain" (1 Corinthians 15:58).

It can be scary taking that first step of faith, but Wendi took the initiative in declaring her faith to her coworkers. Now she has a ministry of prayer.

Willingly give your efforts to God. He will guide you into joyful service to Him. The results will be more than you ever imagined.

HIS WORD
"I will instruct you and teach you in the way you should go; I will counsel you and watch over you" (Psalm 32:8).

MY PART
My friend, don't wait for someone else to initiate something God has placed on your heart to do. If He has told you of a need, then He will provide you with the strength and resources to do it. Most importantly, He will bless your efforts.

MY STUDY
Isaiah 30:21; John 16:13

Cheryl and Susan were college roommates. One Sunday, Cheryl came home from church to find something unusual going on—Susan was serving lunch to an elderly man. Having no family, he lived in a small, trash-filled motel room. Susan had befriended him and was helping to take care of some of his needs.

Acts of Kindness

Cheryl was surprised to learn that Susan had been helping this man for months. She had not known anything about these acts of kindness. Susan hadn't told anyone because she wanted to do something for Christ that no one knew about. She wanted to keep her motivation pure and untainted by pride.

Matthew 6 gives us clear direction about being cautious with our motivation when we perform acts of kindness. "Be careful not to do your 'acts of righteousness' before men, to be seen by them. If you do, you will have no reward from your Father in heaven. So when you give to the needy, do not announce it with trumpets, as the hypocrites do in the synagogues and on the streets, to be honored by men. I tell you the truth, they have received their reward in full. But when you give to the needy, do not let your left hand know what your right hand is doing, so that your giving may be in secret. Then your Father, who sees what is done in secret, will reward you" (verses 1–4).

When God puts you in a position to help someone, do it with little or no fanfare. Your work "in secret" will help prevent unwholesome attitudes such as pride from distorting what you are doing. There is no need for recognition from others because God knows what you did. His is the only opinion that matters in the light of eternity.

How much greater will be our joy when we hear God's compliment, "Well done," rather than the temporal praise of those around us.

HIS WORD

"Blessed are the pure in heart, for they will see God" (Matthew 5:8).

MY PART

Friend, you can experience a blessing today. Ask God to show you how you can help a person with a special need. Don't expect recognition or even a thank you. Do it for God, because it's the right thing to do, and because He wants you to.

MY STUDY

Proverbs 16:2; Isaiah 66:2

DAY 25

Marilyn sensed God leading her to teach a Bible study for women. She was hesitant because she felt inadequate and embarrassed by her inexperience. The other women were older and more sophisticated.

Step of Faith

God persisted in His leading. Finally, she thought, *All I have to do is invite them. They'll say, "No, thank you," then we'll move on.*

Marilyn invited thirteen women. Guess what? They all came! Wonderfully, one by one, they each trusted Christ. Marilyn humbly states, "That says a lot more about God than it does about me!"

What Marilyn didn't understand at first was that all God requires of us is a step of faith. He will take care of the rest. His Word tells of His faithfulness. In 2 Thessalonians 3:3 we read, "The Lord is faithful, and he will strengthen and protect you from the evil one." Deuteronomy 31:8 says, "The LORD himself goes before you and will be with you; he will never leave you nor forsake you. Do not be afraid; do not be discouraged."

God is the source of our strength and He provides

protection. He will never leave us. Therefore, we should not be afraid or discouraged. Even when we are afraid, we do not need to let that stop us from ministering in the Lord's name. Sometimes the activities that we fear most become the greatest blessing to us and to others as we rely on God's strength and wisdom.

Let's look at Marilyn again. With little faith and less courage, she took the first step of obedience in faith. And look what God did! He blessed far beyond her highest expectations.

Where is God leading you? What is He telling you to do? Dear friend, will you take a step of faith? God will be with you. Trust me, and trust Him.

HIS WORD

"Have I not commanded you? Be strong and courageous. Do not be terrified; do not be discouraged, for the LORD your God will be with you wherever you go" (Joshua 1:9).

MY PART

"Faithful Lord Jesus, I confess that sometimes I am afraid to respond to challenges. Please help me to step out in faith and trust You. Thank You for being the ultimate source of courage and strength. In Your name, amen."

MY STUDY

Psalm 31:23,24; Hebrews 3:6

DAY 26

Age doesn't limit what love can do. That's the lesson Gwen's father-in-law taught her family one long winter. Gwen and her family lived in South Dakota, and her husband was on an overseas assignment.

Ageless

So much snow fell that winter that Gwen didn't know where to pile it. Sensing things were tough for Gwen and her family, her 79-year-old father-in-law drove 350 miles from Colorado to help. He not only assisted with the monumental job of removing snow, he stepped in as a "man of the house" as well. He helped his grandson build a small wooden car. He even attended a Valentine's banquet as Gwen's date so she could get out of the house and wouldn't be alone. His time there encouraged the whole family.

The Bible tells us in 1 Peter 1:22 to "have sincere love for your brothers, love one another deeply, from the heart." Gwen's father-in-law exhibited this kind of deep, sacrificial love. He also showed that age has no bearing on the principle applied to this command.

Whether you are young or old, God's Word is the

same for us all. We are responsible for reflecting God's love to others. Perhaps you can't do the same kinds of things that you used to—things that require more physical strength —but you can always do something. You can be a prayer warrior, a willing confidante, a gracious encourager, a faithful friend. You could volunteer at a homeless shelter, or call a mother of a toddler to give her some encouragement. Send a note to your pastor thanking him for his servant's heart.

Dear friend, don't let your age —whatever it is—keep you from being a blessing to others. God wants to use you at every stage in your life. God will give you what you need to bless others, and then He will bless you.

HIS WORD
"Is not wisdom found among the aged? Does not long life bring understanding?" (Job 12:12).

MY PART
"Eternal Father, time means nothing to You. You are the same yesterday, today, and forever. Help me to not dwell on my age but to dwell on You who can strengthen me at any age. I want to serve and glorify You for as long as I am on the earth. Amen."

MY STUDY
Ecclesiastes 8:5; Hebrews 13:8

DAY 27

When the Germans invaded France, Pastor Donald Caskie fled for his life. On foot and on bicycle, he made his way to southern France.

Bold as a Lion

In his new home, he had an opportunity to aid in the war effort. Night after night, he helped escaped prisoners of war find safe passage across the mountains into Spain. As it became increasingly dangerous even in southern France, his friends tried to persuade him to escape as well. He simply answered, "I am needed here."

Oh, I love his spirit. Even when it was difficult, Pastor Caskie stood firm. Proverbs 28:1 says, "The wicked man flees though no one pursues, but the righteous are as bold as a lion." Pastor Caskie was "bold as a lion." When everyone else was fleeing, he understood God's call on his life, and he fulfilled it.

Pastor Caskie was a wonderful example of the kind of determination Paul spoke of in Acts 20:24: "I consider my life worth nothing to me, if only I may finish the race and complete the task the Lord Jesus has given me —the task of testifying to the gospel of God's grace." All around him was chaos and destruction and he was encouraged to leave. Yet he did not retreat from the task God had given him—seeing others to safety.

Friend, we all have tasks. We all are needed. Whether it's rearing children with integrity, helping at a crisis pregnancy center in your community, or sharing God's love on a foreign mission field, stand firm in doing God's work. Many times, you may feel discouraged or even afraid, but call on God for your strength and courage. Keep your eyes focused on Him rather than on your situation. Be "bold as a lion" and "complete the task the Lord Jesus has given [you]."

HIS WORD
"When I called, you answered me; you made me bold and stouthearted" (Psalm 138:3).

MY PART
"Lord Jesus, I want to be as bold as a lion as I minister in Your name. As I work on the tasks You set before me, help me to be diligent and to persevere to complete these humble deeds. In Your holy name, amen."

MY STUDY
2 Samuel 22:33,34; 2 Timothy 4:6–8

It was a rainy night during the racially turbulent '60s. An older black woman was stranded with car trouble on an Alabama highway. When she bravely flagged down a car, a young white man stopped to help her. After he had finished repairing her car, she thanked him and wrote down his address.

The Good Samaritan

A week later, a gift arrived at his home. The note attached to it read: "Thank you so much for assisting me ...Because of you, I was able to make it to my dying husband's bedside just before he passed away. God bless you for helping me." Signed, "Mrs. Nat King Cole."

In the parable of the Good Samaritan (Luke 10:25–37), someone asked Jesus, "Who is my neighbor?" In response, Jesus told him a story. A man traveling from Jerusalem to Jericho was attacked by robbers and left for dead. At least two people, a priest and a Levite, passed by the wounded man without offering assistance. Then a Samaritan came by. He selflessly tended to the man's wounds, used his donkey to take the man to an inn, and paid for the man's lodgings while he recovered.

At the end of the story, Jesus gave this command: "Go and do likewise."

There are people all around us who have been wounded—physically, emotionally, or spiritually. In the parable, Jesus shows us that we must not only help those close to us, we are to help *anyone* we encounter who is in need. If God has placed us in a circumstance to know of a need in someone's life, it is God's will that we assist them as we are able.

Dear friend, the next time you become aware of someone in need and you have the means to help that person, it isn't necessary to ask what God's will is. You already know it: "Go and do likewise."

HIS WORD

"Praise be to the God and Father of our Lord Jesus Christ, the Father of compassion and the God of all comfort, who comforts us in all our troubles, so that we can comfort those in any trouble with the comfort we ourselves have received from God" (2 Corinthians 1:3,4).

MY PART

Someone around you is in trouble. Perhaps a spouse has left or a child is rebelling. Maybe this person is depressed or has an eating disorder. Don't pass them by, friend. Tend to their wounds and help them to safety. It's what Jesus would want you to do.

MY STUDY
Psalm 119:76; Isaiah 61:1,2

DAY 29

William Wilberforce was twenty-one when he began his celebrated political career. When he became a member of Parliament in 1780, his closest friend and confidant was the young Prime Minister William Pitt. Wilberforce was well-positioned to succeed him as prime minister.

Big Dreams

By age 25, with little reverence for political correctness, his heart was on fire for an unpopular mission. Even the temptation to become prime minister would not deter him.

He recorded this life-calling in his personal diary, simply saying, "God Almighty has set before me two great objects. The suppression of the slave trade and the reformation of manners."

England in the early nineteenth century was fueled by the economic benefits derived from slave trading. This heinous practice generated millions of pounds sterling and reached to the fashionable country homes of the aristocracy.

Imagine the audacity of this young member of Parliament! To think that he could alter the economic base of England and transform the civil and moral climate of his times by "the reformation of manners."

Forty-six years later and only three days before his death on July 26, 1833, the bill for the abolition of slavery passed its second reading in the House of Commons. One historian stated, "In the process, Wilberforce went from being one of the most vilified men in Europe to one of the most loved and revered in the world."

One person can make a difference! We must not escape into a private world of defeat or apathy.

Let me challenge you to find inspiration in William Wilberforce. Dream big dreams. Fight tirelessly for what is right and true. Pray for our nation. Find ways to become involved in your neighborhood, community, state, and nation.

Let's not be known as a generation of women who stayed silent, but rather, a generation of courageous women, willing to speak their convictions and make a difference.

HIS WORD
"As for you, brothers, never tire of doing what is right" *(2 Thessalonians 3:13).*

MY PART
Dear friend, there are issues for the glory of God that you care about, causes close to your heart. Find out how you can join with others to make a difference for Christ in these areas. Then purpose to devote time and resources in a meaningful way.

MY STUDY
Deuteronomy 6:18; Psalm 33:4,5

A man walking on a boat dock tripped over a rope and fell into the cold, deep water. He came up sputtering and crying for help, then he sank again. The man couldn't swim. He was in trouble.

Are You Willing?

His friends were too far away to help. But only a few yards away, on another dock, a young man was sunbathing.

While the desperate man begged for help, the young man—an excellent swimmer—did nothing. He actually watched the man drown.

The drowned man's family was so hurt by the callous indifference of the sunbather that they sued him. They lost.

In this 1928 precedent-setting case, the Massachusetts court ruled that the man on the dock had no legal responsibility in the accident and had every legal right to mind his own business.

As Christians, are we to mind our own business when someone is in need? The answer is no. When we have

Jesus in our lives and we live according to His teaching, we can't be indifferent to the needs of others.

By His example and His words, He taught us to be involved in the lives of others, to help those in need. To be like Christ, that is our only option.

You may not have the opportunity today to save a drowning man, but there are many ways to be intentionally involved in the lives of others. It's not our responsibility to take over or to meet all of someone else's needs. However, it *is* our responsibility to live unselfishly, to consider the needs of others, and to do what we can.

Remember Jesus' words in Matthew 25:40: "Whatever you did for one of the least of these brothers of mine, you did for me."

Dear friend, a heart held in God's hands is one that is willing to help others in their time of need. Are you willing?

HIS WORD
"Be imitators of God, therefore, as dearly loved children" (Ephesians 5:1).

MY PART
Here are a few suggested ways you can help others: Provide a safe after-school place for a child in your neighborhood. Be a friend to single parents in your church. Drive an elderly person to the grocery store. Give a few dollars or provide food to a family in financial difficulty.

MY STUDY
2 Samuel 9:1–13; Psalm 82:3,4

The Simple Heart

I tell you the truth, unless a kernel of wheat falls to the ground and dies, it remains only a single seed. But if it dies, it produces many seeds. The man who loves his life will lose it, while the man who hates his life in this world will keep it for eternal life. Whoever serves me must follow me; and where I am, my servant also will be. My Father will honor the one who serves me.

JOHN 12:24-26

As I write to you about simplicity as a virtue, I find myself in the task of creating a pictorial inventory of all our possessions. Bill and I have received many beautiful treasures from family and friends, and most of our possessions belong to Campus Crusade. When Bill and I signed a contract to become slaves of Jesus Christ, we committed to not accumulate possessions. Our contract was not an attempt to simplify our lives, but a covenant with God to prioritize serving Him.

Simplicity is not the absence of "things" or activities. A simple heart can embrace activities with a deliberate attitude of accomplishment, knowing that the priorities have been guided by the Holy Spirit.

Simplicity is also not a matter of style but rather an attitude of the heart. A heart surrendered to Christ has a priority that impacts every thought and activity. Compassion flows from our hearts and prompts us to provide for the needs of others. Simplicity of emotions will purify our actions. Words will be spoken more deliberately and anger will be replaced with patience.

The mystery of creation that we see in the season of autumn reminds us that out of death comes life. A falling leaf enriches the soil for the new sprout of spring. Dying to self and living with Christ as our priority eternally enriches our lives. It is the ultimate answer to all life's questions. And it is the foundation for simplicity.

DAY 31

Arch Hart, a popular author and speaker, tells a story of one harried week when the pressures of life had consumed him. Stress was running high.

Going home late one evening after a long meeting, Arch decided to treat his family to a quart of ice cream. It was after eleven o'clock when he dashed into the local grocery store. He was feeling impatient; his tolerance was low.

Slow Down

After he selected his ice cream, he rushed to the front of the store and saw the express line. Then he thought, *This is really crazy. I need to force myself to slow down.* So, instead of stepping into the express line, he chose the next register.

There he stood holding one quart of ice cream in his bare hands—with three people in front of him pushing carts spilling over with groceries.

The lady at the express counter looked at him oddly and said, "I can help you here!" Dr. Hart shook his head. He was determined to break the pace.

The woman with the cart in front of him looked exhausted. Their eyes met, and he asked sincerely, "How are you doing?" They began chatting, and just before she left, she turned around and tearfully said, "Thank you for speaking to me tonight. My life is falling apart. I'm trying to hold the family together, but I'm so tired. I'm so lonely. You may never know how much I appreciate someone looking me in the eye and talking to me." With that, she turned around and walked out.

Arch stood stunned and a bit rebuked, but at the same time very grateful that God had taught him a valuable lesson.

How about you? Are you feeling stressed out?

My friend, slow down. We live in a world of hurting people. Don't let the busyness of life keep you from being a blessing to others.

HIS WORD

"Therefore, as God's chosen people, holy and dearly loved, clothe yourselves with compassion, kindness, humility, gentleness and patience" (Colossians 3:12).

MY PART

The next time you find yourself stressed out by the pressures of life, take a break. Go for a leisurely walk. Put on some soft praise music. Or take a bubble bath. When you are refreshed and clearheaded, you are better able to meet the needs of those around you.

MY STUDY

Exodus 33:19; Psalm 16:9

DAY 32

Most of us struggle with worry, yet the Scripture tells us, "Don't worry about anything." Corrie ten Boom, a model of trust in God, told a story that I absolutely love:

When I was in the German concentration camp at Ravensbruck, one bitter winter morning I woke up with a bad cold. My nose was running. I could not stand it.

Trusting God

"Well, why don't you pray for a hankie?" my sister asked. I started to laugh. There we were, with the world falling apart around us. We were locked in a camp where thousands of people were being executed each week, being beaten to death, or put through unbearable suffering—and Betsie suggests that I pray for a hankie! If I were to pray for anything, it would be for something big, not something little, like that.

But before I could object, Betsie began to pray. "Father, in the name of Jesus, I pray for a hankie for Corrie, because she has a bad cold."

I shook my head and walked away. Very shortly after, I was standing by the window when I heard someone call my name. I looked out and spotted a friend of mine, another prisoner, who worked in the hospital.

"Here you are," she said in a matter-of-fact tone.

I opened the little parcel, and inside was a handkerchief! I could hardly believe my eyes. "How did you know? Did Betsie tell you? Did you know I had a cold?"

She shrugged. "I know nothing. I was busy sewing handkerchiefs out of an old piece of sheet, and there was a voice in my heart saying, 'Take a hankie to Corrie ten Boom.' And so, there is your gift. From God."

Dear friend, use your worries, needs, and anxieties as a springboard to pray. Worry will immobilize you. Trusting in God—for *everything*—will set you free.

HIS WORD
"Who of you by worrying can add a single hour to his life?" (Matthew 6:27).

MY PART
Today, you may be facing one of the greatest needs of your life or maybe you only need a hankie. Make a list of what you're worried about. One by one, confess your worries as sin, receive His forgiveness, and by faith acknowledge that the God who loves you can meet your every need.

MY STUDY
Psalm 9:10; Isaiah 50:10

Ann and Richard made an unusual vow as young newlyweds. Whoever survived longer, they decided, would dedicate his or her life completely to God.

Unusual Vows

In the meantime, they lived a life of prosperous luxury. Ann's vivacious personality attracted a wonderful circle of friends. She bore and reared ten children. She frequented the opera, traveled the world, and gracefully raised money for her favorite charities.

But their fruitful life together ended in 1984 when Richard died of cancer. So, true to their agreement, Ann began to make good on the vow that they had made many years before.

Over the course of three years, she sold everything they owned and dispersed the inheritance to their children. Then, she threw a party.

Eight hundred of her friends gathered to celebrate her sixty-first birthday. She told them, "The first two-thirds of my life were devoted to the world. The last one-third will be devoted to my soul."

The next morning, Ann entered the Carmelite Monastery in Chicago as a devoted nun.

While Ann may have expressed her devotion in other ways, I'm tremendously impressed with her willingness to let go of everything that she and Richard had acquired. I respect her sincere desire to please God.

Ann relinquished what most would hoard—wealth, fame, and a self-indulgent lifestyle—to give priority to the spiritual dimension of life.

I'm not suggesting that surrendering to God means entering a convent or living a Spartan existence. Obedience to God, wherever He might lead, brings the greatest satisfaction. In fact, the paradox is that when we hold onto possessions with a tight grip, we lose our happiness, but as we let go, the Lord fills our hearts with supernatural joy.

Let's learn a lesson from Ann. Let go of those things that you started out owning, but now find that they own you.

HIS WORD
"My prayer is not that you take them out of the world but that you protect them from the evil one. They are not of the world, even as I am not of it. Sanctify them by the truth; your word is truth" (John 17:15–17).

MY PART
"Lord Jesus, You are the source of infinite joy, love, and satisfaction. Forgive me for placing too much importance on the things of this world. Help me to always remember that a life focused on You is the only life I need. In Your holy name, amen."

MY STUDY
Psalm 86:2; Isaiah 26:3

DAY 34

Do you ever get tired of cleaning? The house starts out spotless in the morning, but by afternoon it looks like a bomb exploded!

Our lives are sometimes like that. We get up in the morning, spend some devotional time with the Lord, get spiritually cleaned-up, but by midday, we're a total wreck.

Spiritual Breathing

How can we keep the trash from piling up in our lives? I believe the best way is regular maintenance rather than holding out for "spring cleaning." Moment by moment, we need to tidy up our hearts.

I have learned to confess my sin as soon as I'm aware of it. When I know I've thought or done something that does not honor God, I immediately "breathe spiritually." First, I exhale—confess my sin and agree with God that what I've done is wrong. Then, I inhale—take in the truth of God's Word that I'm forgiven and clean before Him.

When I first started applying this principle, I had two

young sons, a very busy husband, and a telephone that never stopped ringing. Interruptions plagued me, no matter how cleverly I planned the day.

One time the phone rang at an inconvenient time, and I answered with a cheery—"Hello!" The voice on the other end said, "Oh, Vonette, it's always so wonderful to hear your voice. You're always so pleasant." My heart sank. I felt hypocritical. I wanted to appear spiritual, but my heart was far from it.

That day I learned it's better to trust God in the interruptions than to constantly be frustrated during them. I confessed my attitude to God and asked Him to enable me to use interruptions to honor Him. Exhale. Inhale.

Whatever has a tendency to dirty up your house, get rid of it! Sweep it out quickly! Inhale and exhale throughout your day. As you do, you'll know peace and joy as never before!

HIS WORD
"Cleanse me with hyssop, and I will be clean; wash me, and I will be whiter than snow" (Psalm 51:7).

MY PART
Spiritual breathing will help you keep a short account with God. The more you practice it, the more it will become a routine part of your life. Try it for the next week, and see what a difference it makes in your life and your spirit.

MY STUDY
Isaiah 32:17; Hebrews 10:22

DAY 35

My friend Liz was packing for a weekend camping trip in California with other singles. She included her make-up kit just in case she needed it.

When she discovered there were no lights in the bathroom at the campground, Liz realized she'd be roughing it a little. So the next morning as she stood before the mirror, she had a decision to make. Make-up or no make-up?

True Beauty

She debated with herself for about five minutes. Finally Liz said to herself, *Hey, I'm camping! What does it matter?*

So, putting insecurity behind her, Liz walked out with no make-up on. She felt somewhat exposed. Would anyone notice?

Well, someone did notice. One of the single men took her aside and said, "Hey, Liz, you look good without make-up!" What a compliment! What an affirmation!

She learned she didn't have to hide behind foundation, lip gloss, and mascara. Liz could be herself and others would accept her.

In Scripture, Jesus had several encounters with women. He accepted each of them no matter what her background, race, status, or appearance.

The New Testament tells us, "Your beauty should not come from outward adornment, such as braided hair and the wearing of gold jewelry and fine clothes. Instead, it should be that of your inner self, the unfading beauty of a gentle and quiet spirit, which is of great worth in God's sight" (1 Peter 3:3). I'm not suggesting you throw away your make-up or wardrobe. But I *do* want you to examine your tendency to rely on your appearance *alone* for security and identity.

My friend, we are most attractive when we reflect the Lord's beauty. He is our mirror. He will show you who you really are because you are made in His image. You are His child, the object of His love. Concentrate on those things—in yourself and in others.

HIS WORD

"The LORD said to Samuel, 'Do not consider his appearance or his height, for I have rejected him. The LORD does not look at the things man looks at. Man looks at the outward appearance, but the LORD looks at the heart'" (1 Samuel 16:7).

MY PART

Do the women you know seem insecure about their appearance, afraid to be seen without make-up? Make it a habit to be an encouragement to them. Compliment the positive qualities you see in them, especially those that are not physical. Tell them how valuable they are.

MY STUDY

Job 29:14; Revelation 3:18

DAY 36

In the 1800s, John Paton was a missionary in the southwestern Pacific islands. To reach the islanders for Christ, he began to translate the Scripture.

Before long, he ran into a major hurdle. They had no word equivalent to our word "believe." Nothing even came close. For several weeks, John struggled to find a word or phrase to help these people know what it means to believe.

To Believe

One day, a worker came into John's office, worn out from a hard day. He collapsed into a nearby chair. Then he stretched and put his legs up on another chair. As he breathed a contented sigh of relief, he told John it felt good to lean his whole weight on those chairs.

That was it! "Lean my whole weight on." He'd finally found the right words to explain the concept "to believe."

To "lean my whole weight on" brings to mind something I can totally rest in and depend upon. The fact that I can lean my whole weight upon something has nothing to do with the strength of my belief. It has everything to do with the *object* in which I'm putting my belief.

Believing in God has nothing to do with the strength or size of our belief, but it has everything to do with the One in whom we believe.

Friend, when you tell others about Christ, be very clear about what you're communicating. Don't take for granted that people will understand what it means to believe.

Tell them what Scripture says about the object of our belief: He is the Creator of the universe, all-knowing and all-powerful, the Holy One, faithful and true, the Great Shepherd, love.

Lean the whole weight of your world upon Him—your cares, your concerns, your heartaches. That is the essence of the gospel. That is what you need to communicate to your friends.

HIS WORD
"Trust in the LORD with all your heart and lean not on your own understanding" (Proverbs 3:5).

MY PART
Do you lean the weight of your world upon Christ? You can do this by keeping an open line of communication with Him. Whatever you face throughout the day, give it to Him. Let Him take care of you.

MY STUDY
Jeremiah 17:7; Romans 10:10

During World War II, banners were hung in the windows of homes all across America. They were a symbol that a soldier had gone out from that home.

A blue star was displayed in the window when a son was sent into battle, and a gold one was hung if he wasn't coming home.

A Gold Star

One evening, a young boy was walking down the street with his father. The stars and the banners captured his attention.

Before long, he began counting, "One star in that window. And two in that one!" He clapped his little hands innocently and shouted, "Oh look, Daddy! There are three stars at that house!"

Then the boy asked, "What are those blue and gold stars for, Daddy?"

As they kept walking, the father tried to explain as best he could. His son listened carefully.

As Dad finished talking, they came to a vacant lot. There were no houses—no windows in which to hang service banners. But in the distance was a stretch of sky where one evening star brightly glowed.

"Oh, look!" the little boy exclaimed. "There's one star in *God's* window. That means God gave a Son, too." Noticing the gold color, he added, "And Daddy, God's Son died."

Out of the mouths of babes! Such a profound observation for a five-year-old.

He was right! The same way Americans posted gold stars in their windows, God the Father also gave a Son—His only Son. His death paid the penalty of sin, rescuing mankind from the sentence of death and reconciling to God all who repent.

But Jesus' death was only part of the process. For He not only died, He rose from the dead as well, claiming victory over sin.

Jesus, the shining Star, changed the world forever. A simple truth communicated in a powerful way by a five-year-old boy and a gold star.

HIS WORD

"Thanks be to God! He gives us the victory through our Lord Jesus Christ" (1 Corinthians 15:57).

MY PART

Jesus' death and resurrection were for you. All you need to do is accept His sacrificial gift and invite Him to enter your heart. You can do this by turning to the back of this book to Beginning Your Journey of Joy. *This material will guide you.*

MY STUDY

Psalm 25:5; Jeremiah 24:7

DAY 38

When communists took over Bulgaria, Margaret was fourteen.

Soldiers stormed through the city, confiscating all the Bibles from churches, libraries, shops, and even homes. Miraculously, one older lady hid her beloved Bible under her skirt!

God's Word

Not having God's Word was horrible for Margaret. When she was lonely, struggled with life, or needed strength, she had no record of God's faithfulness.

The lady who'd kept her Bible hidden began to feel guilty about not sharing it with others. So one day, she took the Bible to church. She carefully cut it apart, giving each person two pages.

The pages Margaret received contained Genesis 16 and 17 where God tells the story of Abraham and Sarah. In this story, Margaret saw how God provided for His people in miraculous ways. Every day she read her pages and prayed, "Oh, Lord, please provide Your Word for me." It was her deepest desire and prayer for twenty-five years.

After she became a world-class violinist, she escaped to America at age 37. She got out with her dearest possessions—her violin and the two Bible pages.

When Margaret first arrived in Los Angeles, where she played in the Philharmonic Orchestra, friends wanted to buy her a gift. There was only one thing she wanted: a Bible.

"You must understand," she said. "I didn't know this was *not* a difficult gift for my American friends to give me."

They took her to a Bible bookstore. When she walked in, she looked around to see shelves filled with Bibles. In awe, she fell to her knees. She began to sob. "Oh, God," she cried, "any minute now, I will have your Word."

Since then, Margaret has translated the Scriptures into Bulgarian and taken thousands of Bibles into her beloved homeland.

She's never forgotten what it was like to be without God's Word. She keeps those two precious Bible pages framed as a reminder of how precious God's Word is to us.

HIS WORD
"Oh, how I love your law! I meditate on it all day long" (Psalm 119:97).

MY PART
"Heavenly Father, thank You for Your Word. How precious it is to me. The Scriptures are a constant source of comfort and help. The love You have poured into Your Word is made new each time I read it. May Your Word always be available to any who seek it. Amen."

MY STUDY
Deuteronomy 8:1–3; Colossians 3:16

DAY 39

A "C." That's what Rebecca's report card said for high-school typing. It wasn't exactly Rebecca's toughest class as a sophomore, but she didn't like it. She emphatically told God, "I'll never want a job that requires me to type!"

The Report Card

Ironically, a few years later, Rebecca enrolled in journalism school. Talk about typing! Being a journalist required typing under the intense pressure of tough deadlines. But the thrill of chasing the story won her over. Undoubtedly, this was where God wanted her.

Rebecca began her newspaper-reporting career in the days before computers. Time and again, she cranked a new sheet of paper into place, and off she'd go writing her story. Inevitably, she'd dislike the lead paragraph or would make a mistake.

First, she'd try to erase the error or use correction fluid, but they left smudge marks and were hard to use on whole paragraphs. Finally, she'd reach up, rip the paper out, wad it up, and toss it in the trash. Then, the process would repeat itself.

At her second newspaper job, the introduction of the computer was her saving grace.

Now, I don't know much about computers and they seem a bit complicated to me, but Rebecca assures me they've made her life incredibly easier. Now when Rebecca makes a typing mistake, she just hits the Delete key. It immediately erases her error.

As simplistic as this may sound, I am reminded of what God does with our sin. When Jesus Christ, the Son of God, died on the cross, He gave His life to forgive our sin. When we go to God and confess our sin, it's like God hits the Delete key. He immediately erases the sin—forever.

Dear friend, when you choose to put your trust in Jesus Christ, you're accepting His forgiveness for all your sin—past, present, and future. They're forgiven, "deleted" forever!

HIS WORD
"I will forgive their wickedness and will remember their sins no more" (Jeremiah 31:34).

MY PART
"Merciful Lord, thank You for Your atoning sacrifice that made it possible for me to be forgiven of my sins. Thank You for taking them away forever, remembering them no more. Help me share this marvelous truth with others that they too may receive Your forgiveness. Amen."

MY STUDY
Psalm 130:3–5; Hebrews 10:17

DAY 40

Friends of mine, who were traveling in England, found that driving their rental car presented a real challenge. In England, unlike the United States, you drive on the opposite side of the road while sitting on the opposite side of the car and shift gears with the opposite hand!

Jesus Cares

Just a few miles down the road, the pressure of driving was intense. Mary said she had a knot in her stomach, a pain in her neck, tightness in her chest, *and* a headache. She was not having fun!

The quaint English countryside was beautiful, but Mary couldn't enjoy it. Fear kept her from taking her eyes off the road for even a second. She prayed that God would get them safely to their destination.

What Mary really needed was reassurance, and she found it on the side of the road. A small, obscure sign read "Jesus Cares."

Mary said to her friend, "Isn't that dear? The Lord put that little sign there just for me!"

As she got closer to the sign, she discovered it did

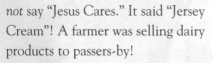

not say "Jesus Cares." It said "Jersey Cream"! A farmer was selling dairy products to passers-by!

We've laughed and laughed about that story. But it was just the encouragement Mary needed. She learned a long time ago that Jesus cares about her. He isn't limited in His ability to assure her of His care.

Jesus is a personal God. He cares about you. He's intensely interested in who you are, what you experience in life, and what concerns you.

Friend, Jesus is moved with compassion about *your* need—no matter how great or small. If it matters to you, it matters to Him. When you come to Him with your need, He feels compassion. And He will meet you there.

Tell Him your need today. Be very specific. Trust Him to do what is best for you.

HIS WORD
"The LORD is good to all; he has compassion on all he has made" (Psalm 145:9).

MY PART
What are your needs today? Consider keeping a prayer journal. Each day record the needs you have, and as God answers, record that next to the request. A prayer journal is a wonderful way to see and record God's faithfulness. Then you can rest assured that God hears your prayers and cares about you.

MY STUDY
Isaiah 63:7; Matthew 9:35,36

DAY 41

Have you ever noticed that our personalities can differ, from day to day and even hour to hour? One day, someone's happy and cooperative. An hour later, he or she may be angry and defensive.

Middle C

Thankfully, God is not like that. He's an emotional God, but He isn't moody. Every day He cares for you and loves you. His love never wanes or changes. It never vacillates from one day to another.

Here's a story to illustrate this concept

While going to college, Lloyd C. Douglas, the author of *The Robe*, lived in a boarding house. Downstairs lived a retired music teacher who was ill and unable to leave his home. Everyday, Mr. Douglas would pop into the man's room. "Well, what's the good news?" he'd joyfully ask.

The music teacher would pick up his tuning fork. Then he'd tap it on the side of his wheelchair. As he held it up, the man would say, "This is middle C! It was middle C yesterday; it will be middle C tomorrow; it will be middle C a thousand years from now."

It's so easy to assume Jesus loves us only when we do good and right things, that God's love is as imperfect as ours is. Nothing could be further from the truth. All we have to do is go to the Bible to know the real Truth.

In Malachi 3:6, God says, "I the LORD do not change." And Hebrews 13:8 says, "Jesus Christ is the same yesterday and today and forever."

Take it from the Word of God. Like middle C, God never changes. So great is His love for you that He gave His one and only Son to pay the debt of sin for you. Show Him you're thankful for His selfless act by *believing* in the unchanging truth that He loves you. He always has; He always will.

HIS WORD
"I am the Alpha and the Omega, the First and the Last, the Beginning and the End" (Revelation 22:13).

MY PART
"Heavenly Father, Your unchanging nature is a constant source of security for me. Amid the ever-changing nature of life, You alone are the rock to which I can cling. Because You never change, my future is secure and eternal. I love you. Amen."

MY STUDY
Psalm 102:25–27; Malachi 3:6

DAY 42

There's one thing many Americans will do once a year that they won't do at any other time. As families gather at Thanksgiving, for an awkward moment they will bow their heads to give thanks to God. The prayer will then give way to food, football, and family frolic.

Saying Grace

Few people pause to truly give heartfelt thanks. But it wasn't too many years ago that saying grace—returning thanks—was as routine as the meal itself. Families ate together, and no one started eating before grace was said. Today, we're often surprised when we see someone in a restaurant pause to give thanks, although it's only a simple acknowledgment of God's provision.

Everyone experiences happy times and sad times, good times and bad, joy and sorrow. That's the way life is. Maybe Thanksgiving Day is nothing more than a painful reminder of how difficult your life is right now. So perhaps you don't feel like there's much to be thankful for. Even saying thanks for a meal is too much.

In 1 Thessalonians 5:18, God tells us to "give thanks in all circumstances, for this is God's will for you in

Christ Jesus."

Dear friend, God knows all about your life. He knows what you're going through. As strange as it may seem, God wants you to express thanks for those desperate times. When you do, you're saying to Him, "I trust You." There's nothing more pleasing to Him than when we choose to trust Him for *everything*.

Express your trust in Him by saying "thank you." Begin with simple things like grace at mealtime. When you begin giving thanks in the little things, you'll find it easier to be thankful for *everything*.

When you bow your head at the Thanksgiving table, ask God to remind you daily to pause and give thanks for your meals. As you do, you'll see *His grace* in your life.

HIS WORD
"Then he took the seven loaves and the fish, and when he had given thanks, he broke them and gave them to the disciples, and they in turn to the people" (Matthew 15:36).

MY PART
This morning when you reached down to slip on your shoes, did you remember that He provided those for you? What about the snack you fixed to tide you over until dinner? God provided that, too. As you go through your day, notice the little blessings, and pause to thank God for each one.

MY STUDY
1 Chronicles 16:8; Psalm 7:17

DAY 43

It was four o'clock in the morning when nine soldiers with machine guns burst into the home of my friends serving Christ in their native Middle Eastern country. The soldiers ransacked every room looking for evidence of Christian ministry.

Unbelievably, the terrified woman offered to serve the soldiers tea.

A Cup of Tea

They took her husband into custody and ordered him to stop his ministry work. With God's strength and grace, he told the soldiers, "No." He would never stop telling others about Jesus Christ.

The soldiers then showed him graphic pictures of the torture they'd inflict to force him into compliance. Again they asked if he'd stop. He answered, "No. And even if you take me to jail, I'll tell people *there* about Christ. If you let me go, *on the outside* I'll tell people about Christ."

The soldiers were perplexed about what to do. After some thought, one finally said, "We noticed your wife is pregnant, so we'll let you go." This soldier was one to whom the wife had served tea. His heart had been softened.

However, the family was put under strict surveillance for the next six months. Everyone who came to their home was interrogated, so eventually people stopped coming. Although alone and isolated, the family kept their faith and consistently demonstrated the love of Christ.

One day, one of the most brutal interrogators came to their home asking for prayer. The soldier's pregnant wife had fallen down, causing her to lose the baby. Also, his young son had developed a potentially fatal skin disease.

Part of this soldier's job was to read confiscated materials. As a result of reading one of the books, he placed his faith in Jesus Christ. Today, he's become one of this family's best friends.

God began with a godly woman simply serving a cup of tea and ended with another soul for the kingdom.

HIS WORD

"If your enemy is hungry, give him food to eat; if he is thirsty, give him water to drink" (Proverbs 25:21).

MY PART

The amazing thing about kindness is that it never comes back void. The blessings from your kind act can come when you least expect them. Even if the act is not reciprocated, the joy you receive from blessing someone else is immeasurable.

MY STUDY

2 Samuel 24:14; Matthew 5:42–44

DAY 44

In the 1950s, Jim Elliot was martyred in Ecuador by primitive Auca Indians as he took the message of Christ to them. He was a young man whose life was completely committed to God. As a student at Wheaton College, the dean asked Jim to write a letter to his fellow students about what it means to "live Christ" during his vacation.

Wise Words

Although Jim's letter was written 49 years ago, it's amazingly relevant to us today.

He pinpoints two concerns about having time away from our routine: activity and inactivity. About *activity*, he says we have to be careful that parties and socializing, even doing good things, don't take the place of our quiet time with the Lord.

He wrote, "For the disciples it was the crowd that set up a barrier to quiet recuperation. This is what I mean by activity—the very need of those we are to contact becomes a snare that gives us occasion to neglect the sacred, secret [times] with Christ, which alone can fit us to fill that need."

Here is what Jim says about *inactivity*: "The let-down

of an unscheduled period where no bells ring, no assignments come due … tends to make us yawn-happy and will often keep us in bed, yielding to undisciplined sloth … Consider the main gripe against spending time in prayer and Bible study: 'I just haven't got time.' No, but when vacation comes, we suddenly forget that we actually have time and use it to catch up on our sleep rather than on our Bible study."

What an exhortation to us! Dear friend, spend time with God. You will be changed by even a few minutes of prayer and reading His Word each day. Have you spent time with Him today? Do it now before other distractions crowd out that all-important meeting.

HIS WORD

"When you pray, go into your room, close the door and pray to your Father, who is unseen. Then your Father, who sees what is done in secret, will reward you" (Matthew 6:6).

MY PART

The next time you have a vacation, take action to incorporate into your schedule quiet times with God. If you are away from home, perhaps you could find a beautiful spot outside, a quiet place of refuge for meeting with God.

MY STUDY

1 Samuel 1:26–28; Psalm 88:13

DAY 45

A friend of mine hosted two 16-year-old Japanese girls. They came to Orlando to learn to speak conversational English.

Little Evangelist

My friend's daughter, Meagan, was seven. They'd never hosted exchange students before, although they'd opened their home to many guests. This time their guests were nonbelievers. My friend explained to Meagan that most of the people in Japan do not know Jesus.

The girls went to church with their host family. The family helped them follow the format for worship and turn to readings in their Japanese/English New Testaments. In the car following the worship service, Reiko said she was surprised to see the word "ghost" in the Bible. My friend shot a puzzled look in her husband's direction as if to say, "How do you explain that one?"

Meagan, wedged between Reiko and Yoko in the back seat, took the challenge and started talking about God being three persons in one: "God the Father, God the Son, and God the Holy Spirit. You have to believe in Jesus and know Him so you'll go to heaven. If you don't believe in Jesus, you'll go to hell."

That was more blunt than my friend would've said it. She squirmed uncomfortably in her seat. But her husband winked and said to his wife, "Let her talk. She's a little evangelist." Coming from a child in her sweet voice, the gospel was presented non-offensively.

God gave Meagan a compassion for the lost. My friend is hoping her adult thoughts and ways never hinder her daughter's natural boldness in proclaiming the truth and praying for those who don't know God.

Children have a natural capacity to learn spiritual truth. I'm so grateful we opened our home to many guests when our sons were small. We talked about God and His love. Now our sons do this with their children. The gospel passes from generation to generation, just as God intended.

HIS WORD
"Send forth your light and your truth, let them guide me; let them bring me to your holy mountain, to the place where you dwell. Then will I go to the altar of God, to God, my joy and my delight. I will praise you with the harp, O God, my God" (Psalm 43:3,4).

MY PART
Do you talk about God freely with your children? Do you explain how important it is to spread His good news to others? If children learn that God is concerned about people and their eternal destiny, they will likely speak openly about their faith.

MY STUDY
Isaiah 60:20; Acts 15:7

DAY 46

ith her Bible before her, Carolyn bent over a table in a bookstore. She was engrossed in the prayer she was writing in her journal. Then she heard a barely audible voice. She glanced up to see a very old man standing over her. She noticed that his wrinkled clothes didn't match.

In Love

"I see we serve the same Lord," the man said, smiling. Soon he was sitting at Carolyn's table, making polite conversation. Then he leaned forward and asked, "Do you know what I do every Monday, Wednesday, and Friday? I go to the hospital and pass out tracts. Then I go to McDonalds and pass out more tracts."

His smile never faded as he continued, "I can tell you the gospel in 30 seconds. Want to hear it?" Carolyn had warmed up to the man. "We had a debt we could not pay," he began, "that debt was hell. But Jesus paid our debt, and now we can spend eternity in heaven with Him."

This man was in love with Jesus Christ. No one was telling him he needed to spend time reading his Bible or sharing his faith. He told Carolyn that he's making the most of the time he has left on earth.

Before he left the bookstore, the old man returned to encourage Carolyn once more. "Two things I want to leave with you," he said. "Jesus tells us in John 15 to abide in Him, and we will bear fruit and to follow Him and He will make us fishers of men. Two things, abide in Him and follow Him." Then he walked away. Carolyn believes God sent that old man to encourage her.

Friend, as you abide in Jesus, you will be compelled to follow Him and tell others about Him. In so doing, you will glorify God and will accomplish His work for you while you are here on earth.

HIS WORD

[Jesus says,] "Remain in me, and I will remain in you. No branch can bear fruit by itself; it must remain in the vine. Neither can you bear fruit unless you remain in me" (John 15:4).

MY PART

When people see you, do they see Jesus? Do your mannerisms, words, and actions, however small, glorify God? I encourage you today to reflect on what it means to abide in Christ. Look for someone you can encourage. Be a messenger sent by God to minister to another today.

MY STUDY

Psalm 63:3,4; Daniel 4:36,37

DAY 47

Fax machines, modems, beepers, digital cameras, VHS, DVD, laptops, palm pilots, megabytes, and gigabytes. They're all buzzwords today. Only a few years ago, we hadn't the slightest idea what they meant!

Peaceful Living

We're wearing pagers on our belts. We have tiny telephones stuffed into our purses. We have laptops to retrieve and send e-mail or faxes. Overnight mail. Voice mail. Electronic airline tickets.

The convenience factor is wonderful, but sometimes I wonder: Have these things made life easier or more complicated?

Maybe you can identify with this writer, who eloquently composed this editorial for a major national magazine: "The world is too big for us. Too much is going on. Too much crime, too much violence and excitement. Try as you will, you get behind in the race in spite of yourself. It's an incessant strain to keep pace, and you still lose ground. Science empties its discoveries on you so fast you stagger beneath them in hopeless bewilderment...Everything is high-pressure. Human nature can't endure much more."

Guess when those words were written. This was an editorial in the *Atlantic Journal* on June 16, 1833. Two centuries ago, that writer was feeling what I sometimes feel!

When I start feeling overwhelmed and want to return to more serene times, it's important for me to remember, I don't find peace in the daily circumstances of life, in technology, or in convenience. Creature comforts are nice, but they don't bring peace. Peace comes from God.

Could it be that your family has fallen prey to a life so fast, so pressured, so given to technology that you've begun to place your confidence in hardware? Have you lost the wonder of silence? Simplicity? Surrender?

God alone delivers peace. Ephesians 2:14 says, "He himself is our peace." It's a timeless message.

In the maddening pace of modern days, place your confidence in God, and draw your peace from Him alone.

HIS WORD

"Since, then, you have been raised with Christ, set your hearts on things above, where Christ is seated at the right hand of God. Set your minds on things above, not on earthly things" (Colossians 3:1,2).

MY PART

Consider starting a family tradition of one day a month (such as a Sunday) without media distractions—no television, no radio, no Internet. Make a commitment to communicate with each other and with God. The Holy Spirit will refresh you in the peace and quiet.

MY STUDY
Psalm 119:37; Exodus 12:13

Do you get frustrated by life's little irritants—such as heavy traffic, waiting in line, or mundane tasks? Here are three ways God instructs us to look at even the smallest events in our lives.

First, we are to be thankful. God wants us to give thanks for even the smallest blessing or persistent irritant. First Thessalonians 5:18 says, "Give thanks in all circumstances, for this is God's will for you in Christ Jesus." When God says *all* circumstances, He includes the good and the bad, the big and the small, the important and the not-so-important.

Second, we are to glorify God. In 1 Corinthians 10:31 we are told, "Whatever you do, do it all for the glory of God." He wants us to live to glorify Him in whatever we are doing, whether we are making a major life decision or merely sitting in our cars maneuvering through traffic.

Third, we are to let God fill our hearts with gladness. In Ecclesiastes 5:19,20 we read, "When God gives any man wealth and possessions, and enables him to enjoy them, to accept his lot and be happy in his work

—this is a gift of God. He seldom reflects on the days of his life, because God keeps him occupied with gladness of heart." God not only gives us the wealth, possessions, and everything—big and small—that we have, He also gives us the very gladness to enjoy them. The irritation we feel in life will fade away when we allow God to fill our hearts with gladness.

Dear friends, God is at work, even among life's little irritations. The next time you feel impatient, give thanks to God, seek to glorify Him, and delight in the gladness you feel. Focus on Him rather than on your problems.

HIS WORD

"Whatever you do, whether in word or deed, do it all in the name of the Lord Jesus, giving thanks to God the Father through him" (Colossians 3:17).

MY PART

"Lord Jesus, enable me to realize that there really is no such thing as irritants, only opportunities to glorify and give thanks to You. Help me to look forward to these opportunities and accept them with gladness of heart, which also comes from You. In Your righteous name, amen."

MY STUDY

Psalm 9:1,2;
Ecclesiastes 9:7,8

"Jesus loves me, this I know." It's a simple children's song, yet more profound words have never been spoken.

My friend struggled for years to grasp God's love for her. Her father left home when she was very young, so she did not have a good earthly model to even begin to understand God's love for her. Because of her father's lack of love toward her, she couldn't grasp the depths of her heavenly Father's love.

"This I Know"

For many years, my friend spent time learning how to truly know God. She experienced His faithfulness and blessing many times throughout her life. One day, she was finally able to say with certainty, "Jesus loves me, this I know."

How do we know that God loves us? John 3:16 tells us, "God so loved the world that he gave his one and only Son, that whoever believes in him shall not perish but have eternal life." God loved us enough to send His Son to earth to die so that we could spend eternity in heaven.

Romans 5:5 says, "God has poured out his love into

our hearts by the Holy Spirit, whom he has given us." God fills our hearts with His love so that we may experience life to the fullest. What marvelous love He must feel for us!

Today my friend asks her children, "Who loves you?" Her three-year-old says brightly, "God and Jesus." Then she proceeds down the list of others in her life who love her: "Nana, Papa, Mama, Daddy." This simple phrase is used to pass on biblical truth to children.

"Jesus loves me, this I know..." How? "For the Bible tells me so." The Bible is God's love letter to us. Friend, spend time in God's Word each day and find out for yourself how much God loves you.

HIS WORD
"So we know and rely on the love God has for us. God is love. Whoever lives in love lives in God, and God in him" (1 John 4:16).

MY PART
When you spend time with your children or children that you know, find simple, yet creative ways to make God a part of the conversation. Explain that God loves each of us. Point out God's hand in the creation. Tell how God shows us, through objects and events all around us, how much He loves us.

MY STUDY
Deuteronomy 6:6–9; Psalm 102:18–21

DAY 50

Are you tired and weary of life's struggles? Of the mundane routine? Of your responsibilities? Of persevering through your Christian journey?

Life can be difficult. Sometimes the pressures of the day can seem overwhelming. Sometimes we think, *How can I possibly have the strength to get through all that is before me?*

Our Strength

I have good news for you, friend. Although we tire very easily, we can rest assured that God never gets weary!

Read these marvelous words in Isaiah 40:28–31: "Do you not know? Have you not heard? The LORD is the everlasting God, the Creator of the ends of the earth. He will not grow tired or weary, and his understanding no one can fathom. He gives strength to the weary and increases the power of the weak. Even youths grow tired and weary, and young men stumble and fall; but those who hope in the LORD will renew their strength. They will soar on wings like eagles; they will run and not grow weary, they will walk and not be faint."

Are there times when you feel that life is too complicated, too stressful, too exhausting? Do you sometimes think there is no way you can get everything under control? To combat these feelings and thoughts, remember this passage from Isaiah. God alone gives us the strength and power to face the challenges of each day. Memorize this phrase from that passage: "Those who hope in the LORD will renew their strength."

Oh, weary one, God is our hope and our strength. Because God is all powerful, He can help me with anything. He does not expect us to handle our problems alone. He is our eternal Father. Not only will He renew our strength, He will enable us to fly higher, run faster, and walk longer than we ever thought possible.

The One who never tires will refresh you. That is His promise to us, His children.

HIS WORD

"I pray that out of his glorious riches he may strengthen you with power through his Spirit in your inner being, so that Christ may dwell in your hearts through faith" (Ephesians 3:16,17).

MY PART

"Everlasting God, You alone can provide the strength I need to make it through the fast-paced, stressful days of my life. I know that if I put my hope in You, You will renew my strength. What a wonderful promise! In Jesus' matchless name, amen."

MY STUDY

Exodus 15:13; Psalm 18:1,2

DAY 51

Do you find yourself busy with family? Work? Church? Social activities? Does this busyness leave you longing for a moment to catch your breath? Perhaps you don't even realize how busy you are and how much you need rest. Perhaps your life is like Vickey's.

In His Presence

Vickey was in graduate school finishing a Master's degree in counseling. She was also working and seeing clients. She led a full and active life. Very suddenly, her busy life came to a screeching halt.

Doctors discovered Vickey had a rare blood disorder. She spent thirteen days in the hospital and had several plasma transfusions. But during this period of uncertainty, she leaned on God. As a result, she experienced His presence and joy in new ways.

When she was finally able to return home, she was a rested and renewed woman.

Sometimes we get so busy in life that we forget how to stop and enjoy God's presence. Unfortunately, it can take a tragic event or illness to slow us down. It is then that we are able to reevaluate our lives and reconnect with God.

When you are so busy that you don't know where to find rest, look to the Psalms. They tell us where to find our source of rest:

- "My soul finds rest in God alone; my salvation comes from him" (Psalm 62:1).

- "Find rest, O my soul, in God alone; my hope comes from him" (Psalm 62:5).

- "He who dwells in the shelter of the Most High will rest in the shadow of the Almighty" (Psalm 91:1).

Do these verses comfort you as much as they do me? I encourage you to use your Bible concordance to find other passages on the "rest" that comes from God.

Dear one, only in God will you find true rest. Rest in His presence. Tell Him your every concern. He will take care of you!

HIS WORD
"Very early in the morning, while it was still dark, Jesus got up, left the house and went off to a solitary place, where he prayed" (Mark 1:35).

MY PART
When Christ ascended, the Holy Spirit was given to us as a comfort and guide. No matter how busy you find yourself, God is always with you. You can always find rest when you allow the presence of the Holy Spirit to fill you.

MY STUDY
2 Chronicles 6:18–20; Psalm 89:15

DAY 52

Each year for six years, I have fasted for forty days with my husband. Each occasion is a time of great spiritual and emotional intimacy.

The greatest benefit I have received during these fasts is the personal connection with God. Throughout the forty days, I focus on God and read His Word. Through His Holy Spirit, I am able to process the issues I am facing at the time.

Weakness

One year, I was facing some age-related physical problems. It was hard for me to accept the fact that I could not do as much as in the past. But God helped me to honestly face my limitations.

Our human bodies are limited in their abilities, and over time, they will deteriorate. Even the most athletic people among us cannot maintain the same level of performance throughout their entire lives. Weakness is a part of life.

The apostle Paul had a lot of things to say about weakness:

- "The body that is sown...in weakness, it is raised in power" (1 Corinthians 15:42,43).

- "If I must boast, I will boast of the things that show my weakness" (2 Corinthians 11:30).
- "The foolishness of God is wiser than man's wisdom, and the weakness of God is stronger than man's strength" (1 Corinthians 1:25).
- "But he said to me, 'My grace is sufficient for you, for my power is made perfect in weakness.'... For when I am weak, then I am strong" (2 Corinthians 12:9,10).
- "[Christ] was crucified in weakness, yet he lives by God's power. Likewise, we are weak in him, yet by God's power we will live with him to serve you" (2 Corinthians 13:4).

Dear friend, our weakness is a blessing. It allows the power of God to work to the fullest. Don't hide your weaknesses; allow God to work through them.

HIS WORD
"God chose the foolish things of the world to shame the wise; God chose the weak things of the world to shame the strong" (1 Corinthians 1:27).

MY PART
"All-powerful God, I know my human weaknesses, but I also know You are a God of mighty strength. I ask Your Holy Spirit to control my life and to demonstrate Your strength in my weakness. You gave me access to this power when I became Your child. All I need is to submit to You and trust You. I do, Lord. Amen."

MY STUDY
2 Chronicles 32:7,8; Psalm 68:32–35

seola had one old Bible that lasted her entire lifetime. She lived a simple life in a simple house. She had no husband and no children. She didn't even have a car. But she had enough.

Contented Life

For eighty years, she worked faithfully, washing the clothes of the wealthier people in her community. When she retired at age eighty-seven, she astonished the world by giving $150,000 to a Mississippi university.

With her gift, she said, "I have everything I could want . . . I had more money than I could possibly spend."

First Timothy 6:6,7 says, "Godliness with contentment is great gain. For we brought nothing into the world, and we can take nothing out of it."

Oseola is a wonderful example of living a life of contentment. She did not get caught up in the material trappings of this world. She provided for her own basic needs and wanted nothing more. The money she saved, she generously gave to benefit others.

I don't believe being content necessarily means living at the sparse level that Oseola did. Contentment is about the heart. Contentment is being satisfied, whatever your circumstances and whatever your possessions.

Hebrews 13:5 tells us, "Let your character or moral disposition be free from love of money—[including] greed, avarice, lust and craving for earthly possessions—and be satisfied with your present [circumstances and with what you have; for He (God) Himself has said, I will not in any way fail you nor give you up nor leave you without support. [I will] not, [I will] not, [I will] not in any degree leave you helpless, nor forsake nor let [you] down, [relax My hold on you],—Assuredly not!" (Amplified).

Contentment has nothing to do with our possessions or our position in society; it comes from our security in the Lord. He will always be by our side. Everything else should only be enjoyed as a bonus, a blessing from a God who delights in making us happy.

Friend, be thankful for all you have. Choose contentment. When you do, God will fill your heart with bountiful joy.

HIS WORD
"Jesus answered, 'If you want to be perfect, go, sell your possessions and give to the poor, and you will have treasure in heaven. Then come, follow me'" (Matthew 19:21).

MY PART
"Heavenly Father, You have provided all I need and more than I deserve. Forgive me for placing too much importance on the things of this world. I choose now to be content in You and to be satisfied with whatever blessings You give me. Amen."

MY STUDY
Psalm 73:25,26; Isaiah 58:10

DAY 54

In 1999, death came to Cassie Bernall like a thief in the night. Twelve others also died at Columbine High School in Colorado on that tragic day.

Pointing a gun at Cassie's head, her killer asked, "Do you believe in God?"

Before Men

Her response to his question carried a high price—her life. She said, "Yes, I believe in God."

Seventeen-year-old Cassie had been a Christian for only two years, and she died professing her faith in Christ. Her last words made headlines around the world.

The Bible says in 1 Peter 3:15, "Always be prepared to give an answer to everyone who asks you to give the reason for the hope that you have." As followers of Christ, we are to be ready at any time to respond to someone who asks the reason for our faith.

The Bible also tells us that Christ will bless us for our obedience. Matthew 10:32,33 says, "Whoever acknowledges me before men, I will also acknowledge him before my Father in heaven. But whoever disowns me before men, I will disown him before my Father in heaven." Cassie was presented with this challenge in a way that very few of us ever will be. Staring death in the face, she boldly acknowledged her faith before men. Although she lost her life on this earth, she gained eternity with the Lord in heaven.

In Philippians 1:21, Paul proclaims, "For to me, to live is Christ and to die is gain." When we are in Christ, live or die, we can't lose. Cassie didn't lose, and neither will we.

Dear friend, remember Cassie. Do not be afraid to confess your Lord before others! Boldly proclaim to all your belief in the risen Christ, and tell them how they can know Him, too.

HIS WORD
"We have seen and testify that the Father has sent his Son to be Savior of the world" (1 John 4:14).

MY PART
Have you been faced with questions about your faith? How did you respond? Being prepared for these questions will make them easier to handle. Write down the five most common questions you or other Christians face. As you share the good news of the gospel in the power of His Spirit, you demonstrate the authenticity of the Christian life.

MY STUDY
Exodus 4:11,12; Psalm 51:15

Stress. It's the leading cause of many physical and emotional problems in these busy modern times. Even for Christians.

Eric suffers from stress periodically. When he is feeling overwhelmed by the pressures of life, his observant wife can read the signs in his demeanor and actions. To help relieve his stress, she first hugs him. Then, she gently suggests he spend some time with God.

Day by Day

Often, his first response to her suggestion is to list all the things he needs to do and to tell her that he doesn't have time. Fortunately, hearing these words from his own mouth is usually enough to help him regain perspective. He realizes that when he is too busy to spend time with God, he needs to reevaluate his priorities. He is living life in his own strength without dependence on God.

Eric's wife has the right idea. When we are stressed, we need to go to God. Jesus wants to live His life in and through us. He is the cure for stress. He says in Matthew 6:31–34: "Do not worry, saying, 'What shall we eat?' or 'What shall we drink?' or 'What shall we wear?' For the

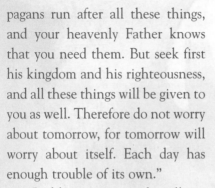

pagans run after all these things, and your heavenly Father knows that you need them. But seek first his kingdom and his righteousness, and all these things will be given to you as well. Therefore do not worry about tomorrow, for tomorrow will worry about itself. Each day has enough trouble of its own."

God knows our needs—all our needs. All we need to do is to submit to Him. That is a sure way to alleviate the stress and worry we feel. As our eyes turn to Him, they will turn away from the stress.

Dear friend, give God daily priority in your life. He doesn't want to be your helper. He wants to live His life in and through you. Let Him control your life as you tell Him about the tasks before you, and let Him set your priorities.

HIS WORD
"Ask and it will be given to you; seek and you will find; knock and the door will be opened to you. For everyone who asks receives; he who seeks finds; and to him who knocks, the door will be opened" (Matthew 7:7,8).

MY PART
We all face stress. Take preemptive measures to prevent stress from becoming overwhelming. Seek God first for every need—social, physical, emotional, and spiritual. Then rest in the security that He is in control of it all. If stress does creep in, go to God with your concerns. He will help you.

MY STUDY
Deuteronomy 4:29; Psalm 20:4,5

DAY 56

The Leaman family was taking a long road trip. To help keep harmony, one of the days was declared "kindness day."

After drawing names, family members were to be especially kind to that person all day, *without telling anyone* who it was. This ingenuous plan was a great success! Kindness and harmony ruled the day.

Kindness Day

The next day, son Durelle suggested another "kindness day." Again, the names were put into a hat and each family member drew a name. As the day went on, it wasn't long until they noticed everyone was being kind to Durelle. The ingenious young man had put his name on every slip of paper in the hat!

That story is not only charming, it illustrates an important spiritual virtue—kindness.

Friend, the Bible tells us that kindness is evidence of the Holy Spirit's control in our lives. Galatians 5:22 says, "The fruit of the Spirit is love, joy, peace, patience, kindness, goodness, faithfulness, gentleness and self-control." The Holy Spirit living within is shown to others through the fruit of the Spirit. Kindness should be a part of our very nature as believers in Christ.

We can also see our responsibility to be kind in Colossians 3:12, which says, "As God's chosen people, holy and dearly loved, clothe yourselves with compassion, kindness, humility, gentleness and patience." We are to wear kindness like clothing, which is worn every day, for all to see.

Kindness benefits the recipient by meeting a need and allowing Christ's love to be expressed through us. Kindness also promotes harmony, where perhaps there would be none.

Dear friend, make every day "kindness day." Give an encouraging word. Lend a helping hand. Provide a shoulder to cry on. Forgive when you are wronged. As you allow the Holy Spirit's kindness to be expressed through you each day, you will be surprised at the wonderful effects—on others and yourself.

HIS WORD
"Perfume and incense bring joy to the heart, and the pleasantness of one's friend springs from his earnest counsel" (Proverbs 27:9).

MY PART
"Father, allow Your spirit of kindness to be expressed through me this day and every day. Show me how to best minister to others, perhaps making someone's day special today. In Your Son's loving name, amen."

MY STUDY
Genesis 50:15–21; Romans 12:15–17

Pastor Donald Caskie was a German prisoner during World War II. The day before his scheduled execution, he asked to take communion.

A German chaplain in the camp met with him. He even remembered Caskie's name from years earlier.

One Good Deed

Ironically, the two men—now on opposite sides of this monumental human conflict—had crossed paths before the war. Pastor Caskie had graciously allowed this German chaplain's congregation to use his church building for worship.

On this day in the prison camp, the chaplain served communion to Pastor Caskie. Then he promised to do everything possible to save the pastor's life. With God's help, that is exactly what he did. The death sentence was commuted.

One good deed done years earlier meant the difference between life and death for Pastor Caskie. The German chaplain remembered the kindness shown to his congregation by granting the use of Pastor Caskie's church building. Despite the fact that they were enemies in this earthly war, the chaplain only saw the grace shown him and felt the need to reciprocate.

The Bible tells us in Galatians 6:9, "Let us not become weary in doing good, for at the proper time we will reap a harvest if we do not give up."

Pastor Caskie most likely did not realize years earlier exactly what his good deed would mean. His generosity was simply an outgrowth of a life led in service to Christ and His principles. When he needed it most, he reaped a reward of his very own life.

Friend, make it a lifestyle to do good to others. With whatever God has entrusted to you, be generous, gracious, and giving to others. You never know just how important one good deed will be.

And even if your good deeds go unrecognized for the moment, keep on working as unto the Lord. God knows! And He will reward your faithfulness.

HIS WORD
"Tell the righteous it will be well with them, for they will enjoy the fruit of their deeds" (Isaiah 3:10).

MY PART
Kindness is a fruit of the Spirit. To live a life of generosity and graciousness, we must rely on the enabling of the Holy Spirit within us. Our natural tendency is to preserve our self interests. Let God, the Holy Spirit, empower you each day to put others before yourself. Then kindness toward others will flow from your heart.

MY STUDY
Psalm 141:3,4;
Hebrews 10:24,25

Rebecca Manly Pippert, in her book *Out of the Salt Shaker*, tells the story of Bill. He became a Christian in college, and he loved the Lord. But Bill had the odd habit of always going barefoot—rain, sleet, or snow!

God's Eyes

One Sunday, he decided to attend worship at a church near campus that was composed of well-dressed, middle-class members. When Bill, barefoot and in jeans, entered the church, he walked down to the front to look for a seat. Finding none, he simply sat on the floor.

With all eyes on the impending situation, an elderly man walked down the aisle toward the boy. This promised to be an interesting confrontation!

When the man reached Bill, he leaned over. Guess what he did next? He sat down next to Bill! They worshiped together on the floor! I love that.

Can you imagine what Jesus would have done in this situation? In His day, people complained that He hung around with "the wrong crowd." But He loved them as much as He loved "the right crowd." I believe

Jesus would have sat on the floor alongside Bill and his new elderly friend!

God does not want us to discriminate against those who look different or act different. God wants us to look inside a person—at the heart. No matter what the person looks like, he or she is loved by God. We are commanded to love as Christ loved. Christ looks at the heart of a person; so must we.

What is it about people that puts you off? Out-of-fashion clothing? Uncultured speech? Unkempt appearance?

Next time you're inclined to judge someone who looks different from you and your friends, remember to look at them with God's eyes and with God's heart. Love others as He does.

HIS WORD
"If you show special attention to the man wearing fine clothes and say, 'Here's a good seat for you,' but say to the poor man, 'You stand there' or 'Sit on the floor by my feet,' have you not discriminated among yourselves and become judges with evil thoughts?" (James 2:3,4).

MY PART
"Lord Jesus, forgive me for looking at others with eyes of judgment. Your love surpasses all our human differences. Help me to see people as You see them, and to love them with Your love. In Your wonderful name, amen."

MY STUDY
Deuteronomy 10:17,18; Psalm 84:9,10

DAY 59

Have you ever stopped to consider how simple the gospel message really is? Think about the death of Christ. The fact is, on that cross at Calvary, Jesus shed His blood for us to forgive our sin and give us eternal life.

The Simple Truth

The simplicity of the message was made real to me one day when my grandchildren were coloring. Keller, who was four-and-a-half years old, colored his page red. Then he matter-of-factly said, "This is Jesus' blood." Noel, who was only three years old, chimed in innocently, "And He shed His blood for our sins."

Over their coloring books, these children unwittingly exhorted a simple, yet powerful, truth! Christ died on the cross for us. He was the perfect sacrifice required to redeem us from our sins. Romans 3:24,25 says, "[All] are justified freely by [God's] grace through the redemption that came by Christ Jesus. God presented him as a sacrifice of atonement, through faith in his blood."

Simple doesn't mean cheap. Christ gave it all for us; He paid everything. Yet the only requirement for us to receive Christ's atonement for our sin is that we accept His freely given sacrifice and receive Him as our Savior. Jesus did the hard part more than two thousand years ago.

Oftentimes, I find that we try to make things more complicated than they are. Perhaps you have even heard someone say, "There must be more to it. Nothing is ever free. There's always a catch."

Dear friend, a gift has been offered to us. There are no strings attached. All we have to do is receive it. It's as simple as that.

There is no "catch"—only the unfathomable love of a righteous God trying to reach out to His creation. There is no need to question this gift; just praise God for it and tell others about the ease of receiving it.

HIS WORD
"I pray that you may be active in sharing your faith, so that you will have a full understanding of every good thing we have in Christ" (Philemon 1:6).

MY PART
To make sharing Christ easier, the truth of the gospel message has been presented in Beginning Your Journey of Joy. You will find it reprinted in the back of this book. Use it to help you learn how to present God's plan of salvation. Ask God for opportunities to share the gospel with others.

MY STUDY
Psalm 13:5,6; Zechariah 9:9

An eight-year-old boy had a younger sister with leukemia. Without a blood transfusion, she would surely die.

His parents explained to the boy that if his blood was compatible with hers, he might be able to supply the transfusion. He agreed to have his blood tested, and it was a good match.

The Transfusion

They told him that giving his sister a pint of his blood could be her only chance for living. He said he'd have to think about that overnight.

The next day, he said he was willing to donate the blood. So his parents took him to the hospital where he was put on a gurney beside his six-year-old sister. Both of them were hooked up to IVs.

As a pint of blood was withdrawn from the boy, it was immediately run into the girl's IV. The boy lay silently on his gurney.

When the doctor came over to see how he was doing, the boy opened his eyes and, in all sincerity, said, "Doctor, how soon until I start to die?"

The little boy had not understood that he was only

giving a little of his blood to his sister. He thought he had to give it all. He was prepared to give his life.

What a wonderful story of love! This little boy was given the gift of life, and he was willing to give it away so that his little sister would live.

Friend, I'm convinced that many of us are falling short. We have received the most precious gift of all—life through Jesus Christ. Yet we're reticent to share that gift by telling others.

We may be giving money, but like the little boy, we need to give blood—to share straight from our heart. We need to tell others how Jesus changes lives through His personal touch—and about our eternal future through His blood.

Changing lives requires active, sacrificial love—a transfusion. We all have something to give.

HIS WORD
"In fact, the law requires that nearly everything be cleansed with blood, and without the shedding of blood there is no forgiveness" (Hebrews 9:22).

MY PART
Perhaps you give money to your church or charities, but what do you give of your time, talents, or heart? Money is important, but a life invested is eternally significant. The next time you hear about someone who doesn't know our Lord, invest yourself in her life by giving out Jesus' words of life.

MY STUDY
Exodus 12:13; Psalm 51:14

The Joyful Heart

I have set the LORD always before me. Because
he is at my right hand, I will not be shaken.
You have made known to me the path of life;
you will fill me with joy in your presence, with
eternal pleasures at your right hand.

PSALM 16:8,11

If happiness could be packaged, I would have no trouble finding investors. Advertisers can claim that a product will provide happiness for an individual, but in reality, only the individual can truly contribute to happiness. Sports events, concerts, movies, and novels can create moments of pleasure. Cheering for the home team or laughing at an author's well-crafted humor is a fleeting experience.

Escaping from the reality and demands of life may offer a brief interlude with a happy feeling, but all too soon the reality of life reemerges and the deep attitudes of the heart impact our actions.

It is difficult to think of celebrating without a sense of joy motivating the occasion. The planning and preparations required to create a festive environment for birthday and anniversary celebrations may become expected rituals without the heartfelt joy of the giver.

But what a beautiful gift is given to the woman who has accepted Jesus Christ as her Savior. A deep, sustained sense of joy can fill her heart with the realization that every little blessing in life is a treasure from her Creator. The joyful heart cannot be erased by tragedy, stressful circumstances, or everyday routine. Instead, this joy that God gives not only outlasts these problems, it provides a foundation of strength.

DAY 61

When our oldest son was in high school, occasionally he would come home from school and say, "Mother, how do you really know the Christian position is right?" As I would answer his arguments, one point made a lasting impression when others seemed to fail. I would encourage him to look at the lifestyle of the true follower of Christ and consider how attractive it is.

How Do You Know?

Then I would ask him to consider the non-Christian and the appealing qualities in that lifestyle. He would then come to his own conclusion that imitating the life of Christ was the most appealing way to live.

Every true believer in Christ desires to follow the instructions from God's Word; however, practicing those truths is often neglected because Christians do not know what the Word of God says. Without a knowledge and understanding of the Bible, we can let the philosophies of men cloud the purity and wisdom of God's Word. Without the Bible as the measure of right-eousness, we can compromise our position or let others influence our thinking and, in turn, our lifestyle.

Christianity is a living relationship with the person Jesus Christ. However, as in any meaningful relationship, we must work at it. Just as we are available to talk to, listen to, and do things for those we love, so we must spend time in the same manner getting to know Jesus Christ.

The angels proclaimed peace on earth and good will toward men at the birth of Jesus, and as we get to know Him and become more like Him, we can understand what peace really means. The "good will toward men" is the greatest witness of the Christian life to an unbeliever. The heart full of God's joy is undeniable proof.

HIS WORD

"Let the peace of Christ rule in your hearts, since as members of one body you were called to peace ...Let the word of Christ dwell in you richly as you teach and admonish one another with all wisdom, and as you sing psalms, hymns and spiritual songs with gratitude in your hearts to God" (Colossians 3:15,16).

MY PART

The peace of Christ is an added gift that comes when we accept His gift of eternal life. It is important that we show people a life transformed by the Holy Spirit. That is how others will know to Whom we belong.

MY STUDY

1 Samuel 20:42; Psalm 85:10,11

DAY 62

For seventy-five years, communism held a stifling grip on Russia. In this atheistic period, mothers could not tell their children about God and His great love without facing severe consequences. But while God did not have a place in the hearts of the new generations, He was not entirely forgotten.

Fifty Years of Prayer

After communism's fall, Campus Crusade for Christ held a four-day teachers' conference in Samara, Russia. More than 300 teachers learned how to teach a biblically based morals and ethics curriculum.

In one of the main conference sessions, Nancy, a Campus Crusade staff member, listened with earphones to the translation of a Russian speaker. Her attention was drawn to a nearby aisle. An elderly woman slowly made her way into the auditorium and sat down.

The Russian speaker finished. Then an American speaker began. Nancy realized this elderly woman couldn't understand his message. She took her earphones and placed them on the woman so she could hear the Russian translation.

Immediately, the woman began to weep and thank Nancy profusely. Tears streamed down her cheeks as she listened to the message. Nancy asked the woman, Anastasia, why she was so moved to tears. Anastasia replied, "This is the answer to my fifty years of prayer."

My heart is so moved by a woman of God who never gave up, who prayed for half a century for her country to hear the message of God's love. I am so thankful God allowed her to see His answer to her prayers.

The Russian officials didn't want us to have a conference in Samara, a once-closed military city. But the prayers of one woman moved the hand of God, who in turn moved in the hearts of city officials to invite the conference to Samara. Today, many of the teachers are teaching hundreds of students about the God of the Bible.

HIS WORD
"Yet give attention to your servant's prayer and his plea for mercy, O LORD my God. Hear the cry and the prayer that your servant is praying in your presence this day" (1 Kings 8:28).

MY PART
God is the One who answers prayer. Remember, the faithful, though silent, prayers of Russia's mothers and grandmothers would not let God be entirely forgotten. Today, don't let God be forgotten where you are. Pray every day for your community, your neighborhood, your coworkers. God will hear! And He will change lives.

MY STUDY
Psalm 17:5,6; Mark 11:23,24

Holiday times require me to adjust my schedule, and reading the daily paper is one activity I put on hold. I catch enough news to know what is going on in the world, but I stack the papers for another day.

Delivering the News

Following one of these beautiful holiday times with family and friends, I sat down to sort through the stack of papers accumulated near my desk. Many of the headlines reported violence and perversion that made my heart ache. But as I reached the papers dated closest to Christmas, I began to see various articles commenting on the holiday. One national newspaper reporter asked five people to respond to the question, "What does Christmas mean to you?" Four out of the five referred to celebrating the birth of Christ as central to their holiday.

One syndicated columnist stated quite boldly that "the true spirit of Christmas is found in imitating the life of Christ." What a refreshing experience. Secular media may not always be fair or balanced in the presentation of the facts of our sacred holidays, but I am reminded that not everyone paid attention to the Holy Night when God came to earth in the flesh as a baby, either. Jesus was born into a world busy with buying and selling. Certainly, the innkeeper had more on his mind than one weary pregnant woman. Even the reports of angels announcing His arrival to shepherds did not impact some folks.

You may not see your life as headline news, but to people who do not know Christ personally, you may be the boldest print they will ever read.

God has chosen us mere mortals as His delivery system of the great news of the gospel. What a privilege we have to make certain that our celebrations are Christ-centered and reflect His love.

HIS WORD
"As it is written, 'How beautiful are the feet of those who bring good news!'" (Romans 10:15).

MY PART
"Heavenly Father, thank You for allowing me to hear the news of Jesus' birth. Help me to make every day a celebration of His life, but especially during the Christmas season when people are more likely to think about Jesus and who He is. Please give me boldness to share my faith with people who do not know the good news of the gospel. In Your Son's holy name, amen."

MY STUDY
Psalm 132:16;
Isaiah 7:14

Carrie is a single mother of two very active teens. Working full-time to provide for her family, Carrie was frustrated. She really wanted to reach out to her neighbors and to her community, but she never seemed to have enough time.

Creative Gift Giving

In December, her daughter and her friends were looking for a way to share the real meaning of Christmas with their neighbors. Carrie had an idea, so she showed the girls the *JESUS* video—a movie based on the life of Christ.

Carrie and the girls raised money to buy enough *JESUS* videotapes to distribute to each house on their street. Even their church donated money to help with their project.

A few weeks before Christmas, they wrapped the videocassettes in festive paper. Then they delivered the gifts in grand style—Christmas caroling at every house.

When Carrie told me about the project, I was almost as excited as she was! Here was a busy working mother who managed to creatively get the gospel message into many of the homes in her neighborhood. Not only that, but she helped her teenage daughter and her friends experience the challenge and joy of sharing Christ with others.

The quality of the video production was so excellent that several of the neighbors expressed their appreciation for the special gift.

Friend, teenagers may be willing to share their faith but may just need some creative input. Special memories of those times will be discussed for many years to come.

It may not have been possible for Carrie or the girls to share Christ with all their neighbors on a one-to-one basis, but the clear message in the video was sure to plant seeds of thought for days after the holidays. Many months after the holiday season has ended, these seeds will still be growing.

HIS WORD
"A gift opens the way for the giver and ushers him into the presence of the great" (Proverbs 18:16).

MY PART
Encourage your family members to share with each other how God has used their words to reach someone's heart. Enjoy the sweetness of these spiritual moments with your family.

MY STUDY
Isaiah 40:9;
John 4:10

encourage people to record in writing their prayer requests and then record God's answers. I've done so myself for years. It's exciting to see how God guided the circumstances and events of life. Susie, a Crusade staff member, records her prayers and thoughts to God in a journal. I think her explanation of why it is important might be helpful for you.

Remember Your Journey

Sometimes when Susie feels discouraged, she pulls out one of her journals from the bookcase and takes a trip into the past. She might read about the summer she worked as a maid and had no money. She had asked God to send her five dollars for lunch, and He did. She was so young in her faith then; she hoped she'd prayed correctly. Through a tip left in a room she cleaned just before lunch, God actually provided more than the five dollars she needed for lunch. She remembers being astounded that God heard her prayers and answered them so specifically.

Or she might read the journal entry recounting a recent trip to Switzerland. Traveling there had been a dream of hers, and God fulfilled it. It was a business trip, but one day during some free time she stood in the Alps looking at a snow-covered wooden cross, amazed that God had blessed her with this trip.

Seeing the proof of God's love on her journal pages encourages her. It gives her hope when she's feeling dry in her spiritual life.

There's another book she turns to when she's wondering if God is still working in her life: the Bible. Sometimes when she reads God's Word, she feels like she's reading *His* journal. Time after time, God urges His people not to forget Him. "Remember Me," His pages plead, "and remember I love you." His words are a personal message to our hearts.

HIS WORD
"Remember the wonders he has done, his miracles, and the judgments he pronounced" (1 Chronicles 16:12).

MY PART
Today, pick up a pen and grab a notebook. Record God's work in your life, both past and present. Take a fresh look at the monuments of His love. Whether you're in a painful place or a "promised land," remember God has led you safely thus far, and He's with you now.

MY STUDY
Psalm 17:6; Mark 11:24

Just two words: thank you. It's one of the first things we teach our children to say because it's something they'll express throughout their lifetime.

We love to hear children spontaneously say, "Thank you." It is refreshing to be around people who demonstrate an attitude of gratefulness.

A Heart of Thanks

The opposite is true, as well. It's difficult to be around someone who is ungrateful. It is a rude person who takes advantage of another's generosity.

It is difficult to comprehend how anyone could be ungrateful for the touch of Jesus. In Luke 17, Jesus was on His way to Galilee when He passed through a village. Ten men had leprosy and knew of His reputation to heal, so they began to cry out, "Jesus, Master, have pity on us!" (verse 13).

These men were being devastated by one of the most unbearable, incurable diseases. No one dared to come near a leper.

Jesus took compassion on these men, and they were instantly healed. Completely renewed! No process! No waiting period! No performance necessary. No payment. Just complete restoration! They were 100 percent healed.

Then the passage describes how all the men left, but only one returned to thank Jesus. This man fell on his face at our Lord's feet—glorifying God and giving thanks.

This is what Jesus said at that moment, "Were not all ten cleansed? Where are the other nine?" (verse 17).

Dear friend, if you're like I am, you feel a bit embarrassed for those men. We can't believe they had the audacity to flee the scene without a simple word of gratitude.

Then I realize that I often make the same mistake. I don't always go running back to glorify the Lord and give Him thanks for His blessings. But we can change that. Give glory and thanks to God for *all* that He does for you and all that He is.

HIS WORD
"Now, our God, we give you thanks, and praise your glorious name" (1 Chronicles 29:13).

MY PART
Before I knew the Lord personally, my life and future held no more hope than those ten lepers' lives did. My sin-sick heart looked just like theirs. Each time I read this passage, I'm reminded of how important it is to be grateful. Pray with me, "Thank You, Lord, for all You've done for me."

MY STUDY
Psalm 75:1; 2 Corinthians 2:14

So many lives are filled with broken relationships and emotional dysfunction. People are looking for happiness, but so few know how to find it. What is the secret to capturing joy, that enduring kind of happiness that gets us through the toughest of times?

Lookin' for Joy

The apostle Paul writes, "Rejoice in the Lord always. I will say it again: Rejoice!" (Philippians 4:4).

Joy is a command, but it is also a choice.

We have been sold a false bill of goods. We are led to believe that joy comes from personal gain. Happiness is winning the lottery. It's finding that a relative has left us lots of money. It's two new cars in the driveway. But is that really joy?

Paul did not just tell us to be joyful, but he gave us a profound example from his own life. "I've learned by now to be quite content whatever my circumstances. I'm just as happy with little as with much, with much as with little. I've found the recipe for being happy whether full or hungry, hands full or hands empty. Whatever I have, wherever I am, I can make it through anything in the One who makes me who I am" (Philippians 4, *The Message*).

That's the secret. Joy is not found in having; it's found only in the source of joy. That source, of course, is Jesus. He is the One who plants His joy in our hearts. His joy produces contentment and happiness.

Knowing Christ means knowing the source of all wisdom, power, beauty, and joy. Every good thing comes from His hand, and He freely gives to God's children. So, my friend, when you're having one of those days when everything seems to be going wrong and your first inclination is to complain or be depressed, rejoice in Christ for who He is and what He's done for you.

HIS WORD

"On that day they offered great sacrifices, rejoicing because God had given them great joy. The women and children also rejoiced. The sound of rejoicing in Jerusalem could be heard far away" (Nehemiah 12:43).

MY PART

Happiness is the pursuit of all people, yet most people look for it in the wrong places. Don't keep this secret to yourself! Speak out! Share your source of joy with everyone who will listen. Every day, ask the Holy Spirit to teach you what it means to say with gratitude, "The joy of the Lord is my strength."

MY STUDY

Psalm 16:11; 2 Corinthians 8:1,2

DAY 68

Have you ever thought about the words to the song *Amazing Grace?*

Amazing grace, how sweet the sound, that saved a wretch like me.

I once was lost, but now am found. Was blind, but now I see.

God's grace truly is amazing.

Grace is a gift given freely to one who has neither earned it nor deserves it. The gift of salvation was the ultimate work of grace. But God's grace was not a one-time act. God's grace can be seen in the constant love and care that He shows for us, even though we are undeserving of it.

Read what a few of our spiritual leaders have said about God and His grace.

Oswald Chambers: "God is more tender [toward us] than we can conceive."

Matthew Henry: "[God] will wait to be gracious... wait till you return to Him and seek His face. He will wait that He may do it in the best and fittest time, when it will be most for His glory, when it will come to you with the most pleasing surprise. He will…not let slip any opportunity to be gracious to you."

John Piper: "God is gracious. He is not limited by anyone's wickedness. His grace may break out anywhere He pleases."

John 1:16 tells us where our blessings come from. "From the fullness of [Christ's] grace we have all received one blessing after another." The blessings we receive come by the grace of God, from the depths of His love.

Dear friend, this priceless gift is yours. Sing out today with renewed hope, thankfulness, and joy. As you do so, think about the last verse of this wonderful song about grace. "'Twas grace that brought me safe thus far, and grace will lead me home."

HIS WORD
"The law was given through Moses; grace and truth came through Jesus Christ" (John 1:17).

MY PART
"Gracious heavenly Father, You gave Your Son as the ultimate sacrifice as an atonement for our sin so that we could receive the gift of salvation. Your infinite grace sustains us each day. I thank You that this same grace will carry me through until I see You face to face in heaven. In Your Son's mighty name, amen."

MY STUDY
Psalm 94:17–19; Jeremiah 31:31–34

Barbara Johnson, noted Christian author and speaker, has a "boomerang" theory about joy. She flings joy beyond her neighbor's fence, across town, and into the universe. Then it curves right back to her.

Boomerang Joy

Proverbs 11:25 says, "He who refreshes others will himself be refreshed." Barbara refreshes others by flinging her joy far and wide at Women of Faith conferences. She's grateful that God allowed her broken life to become a fountain of joy for others.

When you pour out God's love on others, it boomerangs back to you. You don't have to be a conference speaker and author to refresh others with joy. Choose joy in your circumstances. When you are standing in a long line at the grocery store and dinner needs to be ready soon, or when you call someone and get put on hold for what seems like forever, decide to respond with a smile or cheerful comment. You may be surprised how the response itself, knowing that you controlled your reaction, will create a joyful feeling in your heart. Ask God to restore your joy. Joy will be yours, and as you send it out to others, it will return to you—just like a boomerang!

The key to spreading joy is that you must possess a measure of true joy before you can give it away. Your source of joy cannot be based on circumstances or the attitudes of others.

Knowing Christ brings a true joy that comes from a heart made clean and whole. He is a source of strength far beyond any human emotion, and He controls our very existence.

When you know and believe these things in your heart, joy will flow so abundantly that you won't be able to contain it. It will go out to everyone you meet, spreading the love of the Savior.

HIS WORD
"The LORD has done great things for us, and we are filled with joy" (Psalm 126:3).

MY PART
"Holy Lord, Your mercy and love are never-ending. The joy You have given me is beyond description. Help me to show this joy to others that they may know Your love and joy as well. All the glory, praise, and honor go to You alone. In Your wonderful name, amen."

MY STUDY
Jeremiah 31:12–14;
1 Peter 1:7–9

DAY 70

t was a crowded flight, and I ended up next to a delightful, young executive. She wore the signs of success—meticulously dressed, carrying an expensive briefcase.

Can't Judge a Book

Before long, Sandy began to tell me her story. She left her husband because she was frustrated with his lack of motivation. She wanted him to join her on the fast track of success, but he didn't share her drive.

She began dating other men and met someone she thought was more promising. As she became intimately involved with this man, she discovered he was involved in some illegal activities. When she confronted him, he denied it. Then he promptly dumped her.

Sandy owns a very productive advertising agency. But as we began to talk, she admitted, "I've made such bad choices. I've been depressed for two weeks. I've hit rock bottom. I'm successful, but unhappy. My life is a mess."

After hearing her story, she asked me what I did. I

told her about Campus Crusade for Christ and Women Today. She could hardly believe it! She said, "This is unbelievable! I knew when you sat next to me on this plane that something significant was going to happen."

I shared *The Four Spiritual Laws* with her. It turns out that Sandy was already a believer, but was living a defeated Christian life. So I talked with her about the Holy Spirit and living an abundant, powerful, and victorious life.

Sandy was very responsive. The whole situation had caused her to question the value system she had created for herself. She admitted that she was ignoring what was really important in life. Our conversation proved to be timely. God completely revolutionized and enriched her life.

What a wonderful opportunity for me. And what a great reminder that you can't judge a book by its cover.

HIS WORD
"Do not judge, and you will not be judged. Do not condemn, and you will not be condemned. Forgive, and you will be forgiven" (Luke 6:37).

MY PART
Friend, take time to speak with those around you—people like Sandy who may appear very successful, but whose hearts are hurting, and who crave what you have to offer. You will find that God's message of love will break through any differences you may have with someone.

MY STUDY
Leviticus 19:15; Proverbs 16:21

DAY 71

Shortly before Thanksgiving in 1985, Jay had just finished a dinner meeting in Laredo, Texas, when he was paged for a phone call. It was his pastor from Florida. He said, "Jay, you need to come home. Jeff was hit by a car as he ran after a ball. He's in heaven with the Lord."

The University of Suffering

The grief Jay felt at the loss of his 10-year-old son was overwhelming. He remembered the passage in Philippians 3 where Paul says he wants to understand the fellowship of Christ's suffering. Jay asked God to help him understand as well.

When Jay arrived home, he found a house full of people. Suddenly, he remembered a piece of paper he and his wife, Debbie, had discovered earlier. Of all things, Jeff had written a little will a few months ago. They thought it was so cute that they decided to save it and give it to him when he was older.

Read what Jeff wrote. Just ten-years old, he said,

"When I die, I am 100 percent sure I will go to heaven. I was saved on July 6, 1980. It wasn't that hard to understand, except the part that He loves us all. When I die, I want everybody me or my family knows to come to my funeral. Especially all my best friends. I will miss you all."

Amazingly, more than 600 people attended the funeral, and several accepted Christ as Savior during the service. Since then, nearly one hundred more have met the Savior as a direct result of Jeff's death and his written will.

Jay says that through his suffering, he learned that the depth of God's love is the greatest lesson of all. God cares when you suffer, and He longs to comfort you. No matter why you are suffering, you can find solace in His loving hands. He will restore your joy.

HIS WORD

"Shout for joy, O heavens; rejoice, O earth; burst into song, O mountains! For the LORD comforts his people and will have compassion on his afflicted ones" (Isaiah 49:13).

MY PART

"God of All Comfort, You see every tear I cry and every sorrow I bear. You have a wonderful plan for my life, and I rest secure in the knowledge that You are in control of everything. You are the Source of all my comfort and peace. In Your Son's mighty name, amen."

MY STUDY

Psalm 119:49,50; 2 Corinthians 1:5,6

DAY 72

A few years ago, a pastor friend was in Hawaii on business.

Because of the time change, he was wide awake in the middle of the night and decided to wander out from his hotel in search of some fresh air and a cup of coffee.

Party for Agnes

While my friend made small talk with Harry, the guy behind the café counter, the door opened and several young women entered. It was about three a.m. and the women were obviously prostitutes. Apparently, they were regular customers.

One of them, whose name was Agnes, mentioned that the next day would be her birthday. No one seemed to care.

Quietly my friend said, "Hey, Harry. Tomorrow, let's give Agnes a birthday party!"

The next morning at three a.m., he arrived at the cafe carrying balloons and streamers. Harry had baked a big cake. In walked Agnes and her friends.

My friend and Harry sang Happy Birthday, and

everyone joined in. When Agnes saw the cake, she began to cry.

Harry got a knife to cut the cake, but Agnes stopped him. "Please wait," she said, "I've never had a birthday cake before, and I'd like to take it home to show my mother. I'd like to keep it for a few days before we cut it."

Dear friend, we may not look like Agnes or act like her, but from God's viewpoint, we're much the same. We've all sinned and fallen short of God's standard. We don't deserve anything from Him, any more than Agnes deserved a birthday party and cake from my friend and Harry.

But God celebrated each of our lives when He gave us the most cherished gift He had—His Son. "For God so loved the world that he gave his One and only Son, that whoever believes in him shall not perish but have eternal life" (John 3:16). Cherish this gift and pass it on to others.

HIS WORD
"Above all, love each other deeply, because love covers a multitude of sins" (1 Peter 4:8).

MY PART
When you and I grasp what God has done for us—as undeserving as we are—it changes our lives. There are countless thousands of women out there like Agnes, who need someone like you to throw a party for them! Let's make it our life's ambition to celebrate the worth of people in God's eyes.

MY STUDY
Psalm 86:15; Isaiah 42:5–7

DAY 73

Horatio Spafford was no stranger to suffering. You may not know him by name, but you will recognize his testimony.

Tragically, Horatio and his wife lost a beloved son. Not long afterward, the family suffered a huge financial loss in a devastating fire.

Well With My Soul

Then, a year later, his wife and four daughters were sailing to Europe. Their ship was struck by another vessel and sank within twelve minutes. Hundreds lost their lives.

After reaching safety, Mrs. Spafford cabled a message of two words to her husband: "Saved alone." All four girls had died.

While on the journey to reach his wife, Horatio took his sorrow and pain, his doubts and fears to Jesus. He is the only One who could give peace and hope. On the sea, near where his daughters drowned, he wrote these familiar words:

When peace like a river attendeth my way, When sorrows like sea billows roll;

Whatever my lot, Thou hast taught me to say, It is well, it is well with my soul.

No bitterness. No blaming God for the tremendous losses he had suffered. He said that, whatever his lot, he had learned to say, "It is well with my soul."

Is there a secret to dealing with tragedy? Absolutely!

I believe what brings peace and assurance in any situation is a deep heart-knowledge of God. Not just knowing in our minds, but knowing to the very core of our soul.

Paul writes, "I have lost all things. I consider them rubbish, that I may gain Christ and be found in him" (Philippians 3:8,9).

Not only can we know Christ, but He is right here with us every step of the way, now and for all eternity. Whatever we are feeling, He knows and is waiting to comfort and help us. That gave Horatio Spafford hope, and it gives us hope, too!

HIS WORD

"Those who suffer he delivers in their suffering; he speaks to them in their affliction" (Job 36:15).

MY PART

"Loving, powerful Savior, life can bring pain, heartache, and sorrow. But because I know that it is well with my soul, I know You will give peace and hope in the midst of any storm in my life. You meet the deepest needs of my heart."

MY STUDY

Psalm 119:106–108; Romans 5:1–5

Humans can live without food for forty days, without water for eight days, without air for four minutes. But how long can we live without hope?

A friend once told me about his lovely English grandmother, Grandma Dorothy.

The Spiritual Lifeline

Grandma Dorothy lived a full and beautiful life, giving her heart to Christ in her early twenties. She reared two sons, who gave her ten grandchildren and twenty-two great-grandchildren. She died at age 93.

Because she and her beloved husband brought Christianity into the family tree, generations will serve Him and find their hope in him. But one of her sons, now in his seventies, has yet to place his trust and faith in Jesus Christ. So the day of Grandma Dorothy's funeral, the family noticed a stark contrast in reactions.

For the unbelieving son, it was a day of deep mourning and tragedy. His tears fell from a heart without hope. He'd lived a life in denial of Jesus, placing his hope in success and wealth. When his mother died, the loss was more than he could bear.

For the believing son, however, the day was quite different. It was a time of sadness, but also a time of celebration, knowing that his mother was home with Jesus. He shared her hope, which far outweighed his sense of grief.

Friend, we can believe with conviction that when our hope is placed in Jesus, we won't be disappointed. We can have every confidence in Him.

I like Eugene Peterson's paraphrase of Hebrews 6: "We who have run for our very lives to God have every reason to grab the promised hope with both hands and never let go. It's an unbreakable spiritual lifeline" (*The Message*).

Don't place your faith in anything other than Jesus—the giver of every good and perfect gift! As you learn to put your hope in Him, you'll influence generations to come.

HIS WORD
"Blessed is he . . . whose hope is in the LORD his God, the Maker of heaven and earth" (Psalm 146:5,6).

MY PART
What will the generations after you say about you when you are gone? Will they be able to say, "She trusted in Christ, and that gives us hope"? By your faithful example, it's never too late to instill hope in the generations that follow. Live your faith.

MY STUDY
*Joel 3:16;
Romans 8:23–25*

DAY 75

One of the most memorable events of the 1984 Olympic Games in Los Angeles was the 20K walk. The race included several laps in the Coliseum, distance around the city streets, then a final lap in the Coliseum.

Olympic Perseverance

Soon after the start of the race, an unknown competitor from El Salvador fell significantly behind. Nonetheless, he kept walking as fast as he could. Eventually, the others caught up to him and passed him.

All the other walkers completed their Coliseum laps and headed out to the city streets, but the guy from El Salvador still had two laps to go. As this lone walker circled the track two more times, 100,000 pairs of eyes watched him.

He kept on walking. The crowd began to cheer. There was a sense of shared joy—pride even—that this one person, in the midst of a massive crowd, would stay in the race.

At first, spectators had cheered for their own countrymen. Now they were united for this lone walker.

They cheered, clapped, waved flags, even chanted, "El Salvador! El Salvador! El Salvador!"

The cheering faded as he disappeared from the Coliseum into the city streets to try to catch up with his competition. Later, the walkers returned for their final lap, and the gold medal was won.

Much later, a figure appeared in the Coliseum tunnel. It was the El Salvadoran walker. Four hours after the race had begun, he finished his final lap.

The entire crowd stood to their feet. They cheered. They chanted.

He crossed the finish line! Then he collapsed. An ambulance came along and picked him up. Instead of discretely slipping out of the Coliseum, the ambulance circled in a victory lap. In unison, the crowd cheered.

Dear friend, God has given the victory at the end of your race. Persevere in your faith. The battle is won!

HIS WORD
"Therefore, since we are surrounded by such a great cloud of witnesses, let us throw off everything that hinders and the sin that so easily entangles, and let us run with perseverance the race marked out for us" (Hebrews 12:1).

MY PART
My friend, you may not feel you have the perseverance of an Olympic athlete, but when your eyes are fixed on Jesus, you can finish the race. Keep moving one step at a time. Look to God for guidance, power, and support. He will provide it.

MY STUDY
Ecclesiastes 9:11; Isaiah 40:31

DAY 76

My friends, Norm and Becky, lived in their first home for three years.

As friendly people, they visited with their neighbors over the backyard fence, in the front yard, and at block parties. During those visits, they told stories about their lives. However, they began to realize that they never once talked about God.

The Neighborly Gospel

As Christians, Norm and Becky knew God wanted them to share with others about His love and grace, but they didn't know how.

One day, after having an argument over this very issue, Norm and Becky prayed. They asked God to forgive them and to show them what to do. Just a few days later, a friend invited them to a seminar to learn how to share their faith. That weekend changed their lives.

They learned to use *The Four Spiritual Laws*. It's a short booklet my husband wrote many years ago, which simply tells of God's love and how a person can know God in a personal way.

Norm and Becky began using their home as a place

to share their faith with others. They started talking about God in casual conversations and planned outreach events. The first of those events was a Christmas party for twenty-five of their neighbors.

The evening began with the guests sharing Christmas memories. Then Norm told the story of how he came to trust Christ.

As Norm and Becky continued sharing their faith, many of their neighbors placed their trust in Christ. Now, more than twenty years later, the children and grandchildren of these neighbors are trusting Christ as well.

That is so exciting! When Norm and Becky asked God to show them what to do, He did. And because they were "neighborly" with the gospel, many others are now living for Christ.

You, too, can share God's love through hospitality. All it takes is a joyful heart that is open to sharing with others.

HIS WORD

"Each of us should please his neighbor for his good, to build him up" (Romans 15:2).

MY PART

Ask God to show you how to reach out to your neighbors. Then pray for each one. Invite a few of them over for pizza, dessert, or a picnic. Plan a time of conversation. Tell briefly how you trusted Christ. Then share the gospel message using a simple evangelistic tool like The Four Spiritual Laws, *and encourage them to pray aloud with you the prayer at the end.*

MY STUDY

Deuteronomy 31:12; Psalm 143:7,8

Many years ago, my friend Mary was timid about sharing God's love with others. She said, "I wanted to be a 'mysterious witness' for Christ. I only wanted to tell people about Him if they asked."

Christmas Gatherings

Then Mary met Joyce, a staff member with Campus Crusade for Christ. Mary admired Joyce and her knowledge of God. Together, they studied Bible verses about the character of Jesus.

Deep in Mary's heart, she longed to tell others about Jesus Christ. But still, she was hesitant.

Joyce was at the early stages of developing a concept called Christmas Gatherings—an outreach ministry to friends and neighbors. These gatherings are coffees, teas, or dessert parties designed to tell others about Jesus Christ. During the Christmas season, a person invites several friends and neighbors into her home. After spending some time getting to know one another over coffee and cookies, there's a short Christmas program. Then a designated speaker tells how knowing Jesus Christ has made a difference in her life, briefly explaining the gospel message of God's love and including an opportunity for each one to trust Christ.

Joyce was scheduled to speak at a gathering, so she asked Mary to attend with her and to pray for her as she spoke. It was there that Mary understood how simple it can be to tell others about Christ.

During the next fifteen years, Mary became a Christmas Gatherings enthusiast. When her husband's job transferred the family to Hong Kong, she introduced this wonderful outreach concept to those in her church. Many Chinese nationals learned to reach out to their friends and colleagues using these parties. They're still having Christmas Gatherings today.

There is no greater news to share with others than the forgiveness available through Jesus Christ. And there's no easier time than during the Christmas season as we celebrate the birth of the King of kings and Lord of lords.

HIS WORD
"Therefore the Lord himself will give you a sign: The virgin will be with child and will give birth to a son, and will call him Immanuel" (Isaiah 7:14).

MY PART
On the night Jesus Christ was born, angels went to the shepherds in the fields to tell them "Christ the Savior is born." Hosting a tea or luncheon in your home is a wonderful way to tell others this same news. Will you consider doing this for the people you know?

MY STUDY
Proverbs 15:30; Luke 2:8–20

The barrel of goods arrived for Margaret's family. They were missionaries and that's how their supplies arrived. There was excitement as they opened it.

High-button Shoes

Margaret was only ten years old, and she learned a valuable lesson from her mother that day. Margaret's father unpacked the barrel. When he got to the bottom, he happily called out, "Look, Margaret. God answered our prayers. We have shoes!" Then he held up two pairs of old-fashioned, high-button shoes.

Margaret scoffed at the shoes. She wanted in-style oxfords, not the out-of-style high-button shoes. She cried out, "Oh, Papa, they are too big," hoping she wouldn't have to wear them. But Papa assured her that they could stuff cotton in the toes, and they'd last a long time.

Her loving mother quietly said, "Margaret, we prayed for shoes, and now we have shoes. Wear your shoes with a thankful and a humble heart, for it's not so important what you have on your feet, but it's very important where the feet go."

Margaret realized that she'd have to wear the shoes. But she'd have a choice in how she'd wear them: either with deep rebellion or with a thankful heart.

God knows you. He knows your every need. The Bible says that He even knows the number of hairs on your head, and that His thoughts about you are more than the grains of sand in the ocean. That's a God who cares. A God who wants what is absolutely best for you. A God who will provide for your every need.

Dear friend, trust God's provision and be thankful. Even if what you receive is not what you expected, thank God anyway. In time, you may understand more clearly God's provision for you. And a thankful heart will make all the difference in the joy you experience in life. God is worthy of your praise.

HIS WORD

"Everything God created is good, and nothing is to be rejected if it is received with thanksgiving, because it is consecrated by the word of God and prayer" (1 Timothy 4:4).

MY PART

Today, make a list of your greatest needs. At the top of the page write the words: "Always be thankful." As you pray for these needs every day, thank God in advance for how and when He'll provide. Then rest in the assurance that He is faithful.

MY STUDY

Deuteronomy 8:10; Psalm 95:1–3

When birthdays come or Christmas approaches, what do you buy for the person who has everything? If you're like I am, it can take days, even weeks to find the perfect present for someone you love.

Gift Giver

Through the years, however, I've been helped by some wonderful friends who have learned to break free from the traditional mold of gift giving—creative people who prepare thoughtful presentations that don't always require large sums of money.

One woman's husband had grown quite jaded about Christmas. The commercialism of the whole season had bothered him to the point where he couldn't enjoy giving or receiving presents. His wife knew he loved coaching the local high school wrestling team, and they needed new uniforms.

So she secretly donated new uniforms for the entire wrestling team. On Christmas morning, he opened an envelope that revealed her secret. She gave this team what they needed in his honor. It was their family secret. He was so pleased, and it ignited his passion for Christmas-time. Every Christmas since, they've continued to give creative gifts.

Recently, a friend of mine celebrated her forty-first birthday. For nearly thirty of those years, she'd been a zealous witness for Jesus Christ.

Kim trusted Christ after Debbie shared the gospel with her in high school. Now Kim is married and has four small boys. To help Debbie celebrate her birthday, Kim sent a video of her sons chanting, "Happy birthday, Debbie. And thank you for leading our mommy to Jesus!" Debbie cried. It was the perfect gift of encouragement.

Giving gifts is not about how much money you spend. God gave us the most wonderful gift of all, and no amount of money could compare with it. Remember this the next time you need to get a gift for someone. Give creatively from the heart.

HIS WORD
"How priceless is your unfailing love! Both high and low among men find refuge in the shadow of your wings. They feast on the abundance of your house; you give them drink from your river of delights" (Psalm 36:7,8).

MY PART
There are so many ways to express our love and appreciation for one another. Think of a way to give a gift without ever going to the mall. Plan ahead for birthdays, Christmas, or other occasions. The more time you have, the more creative you can be.

MY STUDY
Ruth 2:8–18; Matthew 6:1–4

This was Michelle's first Christmas as a Christian. As a Jewish teenager, she'd placed her faith in Jesus Christ. Now, she longed to celebrate the birth of her Savior.

The Savior

Michelle's parents were adamantly against her new-found faith. Although they didn't practice the rituals of their Jewish faith, they held it closely to their hearts.

They didn't let their daughter attend church with her Christian friends, but Michelle found other ways to grow in her faith. She read Christian books, met with other believers at school, and listened to Christian radio.

Michelle wanted to go to a Christmas Eve service, but her parents would not give permission.

On Christmas Eve, she went to her bedroom. She turned on the radio to listen to Christmas carols. Michelle said, "I heard them as if for the first time. They were like breathtaking praise." While the music played, Michelle spent the evening alone reading God's Word.

On Christmas morning, there was no laughter in her home, and there were no presents. But Michelle awakened with a sense of awe. Her joy overflowed as she realized she had the greatest gift of all—God's gift of His Son, Jesus Christ.

Michelle's first Christmas set the tone for many others to come. She seldom lets the hustle and bustle of the season rob her of the joy of celebrating the birth of Jesus Christ. She says, "Those years of celebrating alone in my room stripped the holiday of all but the Baby King resting in a manger."

Michelle has learned a truth many of us need to learn: The only thing that matters at Christmas is the fact that the King of kings was born in a manger. He was God's gift to us in human form. What a good reason to celebrate—at Christmas and throughout the year!

HIS WORD
"[Christ Jesus,] who, being in very nature God, did not consider equality with God something to be grasped, but made himself nothing, taking the very nature of a servant, being made in human likeness" (Philippians 2:6,7).

MY PART
God became a human in the Person of Jesus Christ. Our relationship with Jesus gives meaning to our Christmas celebrations, public and private. This Christmas, focus on Jesus Christ —His birth, His life, His ministry, His death, His forgiveness, His deity, His resurrection, and His eternal love.

MY STUDY
Psalm 130:7,8; Isaiah 42:10–12

DAY 81

The birth of Jesus is the most cele-brated of stories, but it is sometimes told very modestly by excited schoolchildren for very proud parents.

Room in Your Heart

Thirty years ago, *Guideposts* magazine told the story of nine-year-old Wally.

Wally was a bit slower than others his age, but he was kind, helpful, and happy. Bigger than his classmates, his teacher cast him as the formidable innkeeper.

The angels appeared in coat-hanger halos, and shep-herds carried walking-cane staffs. It was magical. Mes-merized, Wally could hardly wait to make his entrance.

Soon Mary and Joseph wandered across the stage. Joseph knocked on the door of the inn. This was Wally's moment. "What do you want?" he asked.

"We seek lodging," Joseph answered.

"Seek it elsewhere. The inn is filled," the innkeep-er said sternly.

Joseph kept pleading. The innkeeper kept refusing.

"Please, good innkeeper, this is my wife, Mary. She is heavy with child and needs a place to rest. Surely you must have some small corner for her. She is so tired."

The innkeeper paused.

A voice prompted him from the wings. "No. Be gone," he repeated.

As the disappointed couple walked off, the innkeeper watched. Concern replaced his stern gaze. Tears filled his eyes. The tough innkeeper transformed into Wally, the kind-hearted boy.

"Don't go, Joseph," he called out. "Bring Mary back." Smiling brightly, he said, "You can have my room."

Wally's tender innocence magnifies how easy it is to allow our hearts to be desensitized to the meaning of Christmas. We may have accepted Christ as Savior, but life's activities and demands have crowded Him out. Making room in our hearts for Jesus should be a daily decision. Giving Him priority in our lives is the greatest way to demonstrate our thankfulness for His gift of eternal life.

HIS WORD

"Sing to him, sing praise to him; tell of all his wonderful acts. Glory in his holy name; let the hearts of those who seek the LORD rejoice" (Psalm 105:2,3).

MY PART

"Dear Father, I want to always have room in my heart for Your Son. Thank You for the many blessings of the holiday season. I ask You to help me have a childlike wonder as I share the holidays with family and friends, and help me remember Your gift throughout the year. Amen."

MY STUDY

2 Samuel 22:26,27; Matthew 8:20

It was a nice suburb where everyone minded his own business and went about day-to-day living. But for Joanne, the neighborhood had become a point of concern. She was deeply burdened for the women who lived in the well-maintained homes.

Trusting Relationships

The neighborhood was more than dwellings and yards and shade trees. These women were people with souls, and Joanne had reason to believe that most of them did not know Christ personally.

Joanne decided to work her way up and down the street—establishing friendships with those near her home. At first, her neighbors were suspicious of her motives. But with persistence—going back a second and third time and bringing baked goodies on occasion—the walls began to break down.

At Christmas time, she invited several people to her home for a party. To her delight, quite a few showed up.

Finally, after three years in the neighborhood, Joanne had comfortable and trusting relationships with five women near her house. She had even shared the gospel with them a number of times.

Although none of them had accepted Christ yet, they were quite interested in spiritual things and wanted to begin a Bible study together. None of this would have happened had Joanne not been persistent and patient in her pursuit of their friendship.

One of the greatest misconceptions among Christians is that people do not want to know God. In fact, just the opposite is true! People today are turning to God, hoping to find spiritual solutions to their problems.

There are men and women in your neighborhood who want answers to life's big questions. Dear friend, establish friendships with those around you. Let them see the love of the Savior in you. Then, maybe they too will come to know Christ—the One who can fulfill them and give them peace.

"Whoever is wise, let him heed these things and consider the great love of the LORD" (Psalm 107:43).

Do you know the people in your neighborhood? Take the initiative to meet them. Invite them over for coffee, dinner, or a family barbecue. Above all, be available to them as a model of Christ, demonstrating His love in all that you do. Ask God to help you and let Him work through you. He will.

Jeremiah 33:3; Romans 5:6–8

Celebrate the temporary
Don't wait until tomorrow
Live Today
Celebrate the simple things

Celebrate the Temporary

Enjoy the butterfly
Embrace the snow
Run with the ocean
Delight in the trees

Or a single lonely flower

Go barefoot in the wet grass

Don't wait
Until all the problems are solved
Or all the bills are paid

You will wait forever
Eternity will come and go

And you
Will still be waiting

Live in the now
With all its problems and its agonies
With its joy
And its pain

Celebrate your pain
Your despair
Your anger
It means you're alive
Look closer
Breath deeper
Stand taller
Stop grieving the past

There is joy and beauty
Today

It is temporary
Here now and gone
So celebrate it
While you can
Celebrate the Temporary!

By Clyde Reid

HIS WORD
"Therefore do not worry about tomorrow, for tomorrow will worry about itself. Each day has enough trouble of its own" (Matthew 6:34).

MY PART
Each day is a gift from God. Take time today to refresh your spirit by reading God's Word. Spend time talking to Him. Enjoy His presence, sit quietly, and listen for His words to you. Allow the Holy Spirit full control of your life. Trust Him.

MY STUDY
*1 Samuel 2:1;
Psalm 33:21,22*

Doreen and her husband moved to Orlando to attend seminary. Leaving family and friends was difficult, but when they arrived in Florida and stepped out of the rented moving truck, they felt they had entered a wasteland. The stifling heat was not how they had pictured Florida.

The Blessings Book

Doreen knew they had obeyed God's leading to attend seminary, and she made a decision to be very alert to every way that God blessed them in their decision. Doreen and her husband had trusted God to provide in the past, but this major move brought unique challenges for them financially.

Soon after settling into life as seminary students, they received $100 in the mail. No specific request had been made for the money, but God knew their need.

Doreen decided to create a "Blessings Book" to keep an account of the many ways God was honoring their obedience to His call. She wrote down every detail of God's provision for them that first year in seminary.

Sometimes the entry was as simple as the blessing of "peace of mind" or "confidence for exams." The blessings of God recorded in the book created a beautiful journal for reflection and praise to the Giver of every good gift. If loneliness or frustration brought anxiety, Doreen could always read her journal and be reminded of the goodness of God and His faithfulness.

Long after the seminary days, the "Blessings Book" serves as a reminder to her of how many times God provided for the physical, emotional, and spiritual needs of a couple who stepped out in obedience to His call.

Dear one, God is blessing you every day. He has saved us from condemnation; He provides for our needs on this earth; and He is preparing us for eternity with Him. Give thanks to God for the things —big and small—that He does for you. Let your heart delight in His ever-present love.

HIS WORD
"Every good and perfect gift is from above, coming down from the Father of the heavenly lights, who does not change like shifting shadows" (James 1:17).

MY PART
Choose to accept the blessing of God's presence in your life. I know He is willing and able to provide for all your needs. Start your own "Blessings Book," recording each blessing as you receive it. You may be surprised at how generous God can be.

MY STUDY
Psalm 77:11–15; Jeremiah 32:18–20

Life, liberty, and the pursuit of happiness. Isn't that guaranteed by the Constitution of the United States? Of course, we all know the key word is "pursuit." The manner in which we obtain happiness is very personal. The inward desires of our heart determine how actively we will pursue any goal.

The Pursuit of Happiness

Experts today have created elaborate prescriptions for finding true happiness, yet we know that many people are sad, lonely, and dejected. Talk shows offer solutions to many situations that might infringe on our happiness. In reality, we know that making the pursuit of happiness our life's goal can bring frustration and futility.

When Jesus taught the crowds in Galilee, He gave us the most accurate prescription for happiness. Interestingly, it doesn't include much of what our society would use as measurement. Allow these words of our Savior to mold your thinking about true happiness.

> Blessed are the poor in spirit, for theirs is the kingdom of heaven.
>
> Blessed are those who mourn, for they will be com-

forted.

Blessed are the meek, for they will inherit the earth.

Blessed are those who hunger and thirst for righteousness, for they will be filled.

Blessed are the merciful, for they will be shown mercy.

Blessed are the pure in heart, for they will see God.

Blessed are the peacemakers, for they will be called sons of God.

Blessed are those who are persecuted because of righteousness, for theirs is the kingdom of heaven.

Blessed are you when people insult you, persecute you and falsely say all kinds of evil against you because of me. Rejoice and be glad, because great is your reward in heaven, for in the same way they persecuted the prophets who were before you (Matthew 5:3–12).

When we surrender our heart and life to Jesus Christ, we gain new perspectives on what brings happiness.

HIS WORD
"I rejoice at Your word as one who finds great treasure" (Psalm 119:162, NKJ).

MY PART
"Blessed Lord Jesus, I recognize that true happiness comes from You, not from people or possessions. You want us to give when others take, to love when others hate, and to help when others abuse. In doing this, we gain and others lose. Use Your Word and Your Spirit to mold me into the person You want me to be. Amen."

MY STUDY
Isaiah 55:1–3; Romans 14:16–18

DAY 86

It is impossible to get through the holiday season without scanning at least one magazine that has the ultimate answer on how to organize your time and be "super-woman" for your family, friends, and coworkers. We all know it is not possible to do "everything," and yet we try and try again.

Just Enough Time

For the woman who has a time management plan throughout the year, the holiday season does not bring stress but an opportunity to demonstrate that a plan can work. Basically, time management is thinking ahead, planning what you are going to do before you do it. It encompasses stewardship of your time, talent, and treasure—of all that God has given to you. Time management involves determining what you really want to accomplish and then putting those goals into your plans for a week, a year, and a lifetime.

Many times people feel that a schedule is limiting. They don't want to be organized because they like to do what they want, when they want. Of course, some con-

188 MY HEART IN HIS HANDS

sider this liberating. However, I have found that nothing has liberated me more than planning ahead after seeking God's wisdom.

Time management is not designed to confine, but to give you freedom to organize yourself to accomplish the things you feel are important and worthwhile, and that contribute to making you the person you want to be. Remember to build time into your schedule to take care of yourself.

Time management is a part of God's plan. Remember, among the fruit of the Spirit is "self-control" or management of yourself. When you take the time to plan ahead, you are also consciously setting priorities in your life. The things that are important to you are then given due attention in your schedule.

Be a good steward of your time. God will multiply your effort.

HIS WORD
"The plans of the diligent lead to profit as surely as haste leads to poverty" (Proverbs 21:5).

MY PART
"Father, thank You for a world of order. Your creation is glorious, and I marvel at Your handiwork. Please give me a heart to establish order in my life. I want to glorify You in the activities of my days and share Your joy with a searching world. In Jesus' matchless name, amen."

MY STUDY
Isaiah 32:7,8; James 4:13–15

DAY 87

Three little words contain the most profound statement of fact ever made: "God loves you!" But it wouldn't surprise me if there are times when you forget the *truth* in those words.

In his book *Abba's Child*, Brennan Manning tells this story:

Edward Farrell, a priest in Detroit, went on vacation to Ireland. He stayed with his only living uncle, who was about to celebrate a milestone birthday.

On the day of his uncle's eightieth birthday, the two men got up before dawn. Silently, they dressed for the day. Then they went on a quiet walk along the shores of Lake Killarney. They stopped to watch the sunrise. Still in reverent silence, they watched the splendor and majesty of God's creative handiwork.

Suddenly, Edward's uncle turned and left. When Edward looked up to see him, he was skipping down the road.

Edward called out to him, "Uncle Seamus, you really look happy."

"I am, lad," the uncle replied.

Edward was curious. He asked, "Want to tell me why?"

"Yes," Uncle Seamus began in his thick Irish brogue. "You see, me Abba [God] is very fond of me."

Do you know in your heart of hearts that your Abba—God the Father—is fond of you? That He likes you?

Brennan Manning asks this similar question: "Do you honestly believe God likes you, not just loves you because theologically God has to love you?"

God does like you. He created you. Yes, you do things that displease God. I do, too. But that doesn't discount the *reality* of God's very deep affection and abiding love for you! In fact, it *proves* He loves you.

Remember, John 3:16 says, "For God so loved the world that he gave his one and only Son..." He didn't do it because He had to. He gave His Son, Jesus, because of His great love for each one of us.

HIS WORD

"Both the one who makes men holy and those who are made holy are of the same family. So Jesus is not ashamed to call them brothers" (Hebrews 2:11).

MY PART

Turn to the Word of the God who loves you. Read five chapters in Psalms every day, and you'll finish the book in one month. As you do, write down every verse about God's love. Then, whenever you begin to feel unloved, or that God doesn't care, read through your list. You'll be reminded of the truth.

MY STUDY

Genesis 1:26–31; Psalm 149:4,5

A few years ago, some friends in Orlando hosted a Christmas Gathering. They invited every woman in their neighborhood. Many came. They had an enjoyable time getting to know one another, sharing Christmas traditions, and hearing someone share the real meaning of Christmas.

Neighborhood Lighthouse

The girl next door was unmarried but lived with her boyfriend. At first, she said she wanted to come to the neighborhood gathering, but later declined.

About two months later, very late one night, there was a knock at the door of my friend's house. The young woman was in the middle of a fight with her boyfriend and needed to talk. For a few hours, she poured out her heart to my friend.

She wondered if God was punishing her, if He loved her, if she was in trouble with Him. My friend talked to her about the love and forgiveness available in Jesus Christ.

Isn't it interesting? That person didn't even attend

the Christmas dessert, but just by being invited, she knew my friend was safe if she needed help.

My friend's home is a lighthouse in that neighborhood. Jesus said, "Let your light shine before men, that they may see your good deeds and praise your Father in heaven" (Matthew 5:16).

Think for a minute about the street where you live. If someone on your street needed prayer or wanted to talk with someone, where would she go? If she wanted to know Jesus Christ, who could tell her how? Will you be the ambassador for Christ on your street?

Think of ways to open your home. Ask a woman over for coffee, or a few friends in for dessert. Have a couple over for dinner. Then turn these times of casual encounters into life-changing moments to talk about your relationship with Christ.

Celebrate Jesus in your neighborhood so that all may see Him.

HIS WORD
"I, the LORD, have called you in righteousness; I will take hold of your hand. I will keep you and will make you to be a covenant for the people and a light for the Gentiles" (Isaiah 42:6).

MY PART
Ask God to help you be more aware of your neighbors and to be friendly when you see them. Learn their names. Pray for them individually. If you don't know what to pray, find Bible verses (such as Ephesians 1:18,19) to pray back to God.

MY STUDY
Psalm 119:105; Matthew 5:13–16

DAY 89

The date, time, and place had been set. The team arrived just a few minutes early. They waited and waited, but their Chinese contact never showed up.

Miles and Miles

Chris and his team were missionaries in China. They were carrying Bibles to a specific Chinese contact. But now what would they do? Afraid they were being watched, they walked all the way to the edge of town.

The team stopped in a park to rest, get a drink of water, and pray. They noticed three very dirty, ragged men under a nearby tree. Chris sensed God leading him to offer them some water. As he gave it to them, one man uttered, in clear English, the password—the very password their Chinese contact would have used at the "appointed" meeting place.

Chris's team was thrilled. They were awestruck as they listened to the men's story. They'd been walking for two-and-a-half months from north China. They had crossed snowy mountains, a desert, and several rivers.

They didn't know the country and didn't have a map. They walked by faith in God.

The men could only explain that it was God who had shown them where to go. He told them when to be at this park and to expect a team to have Bibles.

When the travel-weary men saw the Bibles, they wept. Then they gave pure, genuine praise to their sovereign God.

Chris and his team then went the extra mile. They exchanged the clothes off their backs and even their shoes with the three men. Chris said it was an honor to wear those dirty rags.

My heart is touched by the deep, resolute commitment to God by both of these teams. When I hear stories like this, my faith seems so shallow.

My friend, how far would you walk by faith? Our God is faithful to walk beside us.

HIS WORD
"Commit your way to the LORD; trust in him and he will do this: He will make your righteousness shine like the dawn, the justice of your cause like the noonday sun" (Psalm 37:5,6).

MY PART
"Lord Jesus, You are more than worthy of our praise. I am so humbled to hear of these men walking so far, not by sight, but by faith in You alone. Help me to walk by faith in my life. I want to trust You with every step I take. You are worthy, Lord Jesus. Amen."

MY STUDY
Matthew 17:20; 2 Chronicles 20:20,21

DAY 90

I t was almost Christmas, and Lauren was feeling desperately lonely. She'd just ended a romance and had no close friends. Lauren, an attorney in Miami, had achieved much success in her career, but her personal life felt empty.

Enlarging Your Heart

An invitation she received in the mail from someone she'd known in law school intrigued her. It was an invitation to a Christmas Gathering. The invitation explained that there'd be dessert and they'd share Christmas traditions. Then someone would talk about the "real" meaning of Christmas.

Lauren decided to attend. At her friend's house, she heard the gospel. The speaker talked about God's forgiveness. Lauren said she was absolutely amazed to hear that God even forgave *her* sins—those of the past, present, and future. Lauren knew if there was anything she needed, it was forgiveness.

So that day in her friend's home over coffee and dessert, she trusted Christ. She received His complete forgiveness. She knew immediately that this truth was the most wonderful news she'd ever heard. As she looked around the room at the other women, she wondered, *Are you taking this in? Are you hearing what she's saying? This is incredible!*

When Lauren left that day, she sat outside in her car and cried for a long time. Tears of joy flowed as she realized that she really was forgiven for her sins. As she sat in her car, everything seemed bigger, the sky seemed bluer, the grass greener. "My own heart," she said, "had grown about ten sizes!"

Lauren now spends time telling others about this wonderful news of forgiveness through Jesus Christ and how they, too, can know Jesus as their personal Savior.

One believer shared with someone in need. That person then became a believer, grew in the faith, and shared with others. What a wonderful cycle of faith! God will use you, too, in this cycle if you will let Him.

HIS WORD
"The things you have heard me say in the presence of many witnesses entrust to reliable men who will also be qualified to teach others" (2 Timothy 2:2).

MY PART
"Lord Jesus, my Savior, thank You for Your redeeming sacrifice on the cross. I know that there are people all around me who are hurting. Please use me to show these people Your love and to point them to Your salvation. In Your righteous name, amen."

MY STUDY
2 Chronicles 6:24–27; Psalm 25:8

Beginning Your Journey of Joy

These four principles are essential in beginning a journey of joy.

One—God loves you and created you to know Him personally.

God's Love

"God so loved the world that He gave His one and only Son, that whoever believes in Him shall not perish but have eternal life" (John 3:16).

God's Plan

"Now this is eternal life: that they may know you, the only true God, and Jesus Christ, whom you have sent" (John 17:3).

What prevents us from knowing God personally?

Two—People are sinful and separated from God, so we cannot know Him personally or experience His love.

People are Sinful

"All have sinned and fall short of the glory of God" (Romans 3:23).

People were created to have fellowship with God; but, because of our own stubborn self-will, we chose to go our own independent way and fellowship with God was broken. This self-will, characterized by an attitude of active rebellion or passive indifference, is an evidence of what the Bible calls sin.

People are Separated

"The wages of sin is death" [spiritual separation from God] (Romans 6:23).

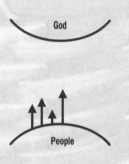

This diagram illustrates that God is holy and people are sinful. A great gulf separates the two. The arrows illustrate that people are continually trying to reach God and establish a personal relationship with Him through our own efforts, such as a good life, philosophy, or religion—but we inevitably fail.

The third principle explains the only way to bridge this gulf…

𝒯hree—*Jesus Christ is God's only provision for our sin. Through Him alone we can know God personally and experience His love.*

He Died In Our Place

"God demonstrates His own love toward us, in that while we were yet sinners, Christ died for us" (Romans 5:8).

He Rose from the Dead

"Christ died for our sins…He was buried…He was raised on the third day according to the Scriptures…He appeared to Peter, then to the twelve. After that He appeared to more than five hundred…" (1 Corinthians 15:3–6).

He Is the Only Way to God

"Jesus said to him, 'I am the way, and the truth, and the life; no one comes to the Father but through Me'" (John 14:6).

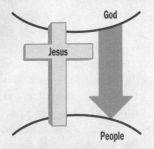

This diagram illustrates that God has bridged the gulf that separates us from Him by sending His Son, Jesus Christ, to die on the cross in our place to pay the penalty for our sins.

It is not enough just to know these three truths…

Four—We must individually receive Jesus Christ as Savior and Lord; then we can know God personally and experience His love.

We Must Receive Christ

"As many as received Him, to them He gave the right to become children of God, even to those who believe in His name" (John 1:12).

We Receive Christ Through Faith

"By grace you have been saved through faith; and that not of yourselves, it is the gift of God; not as a result of works that no one should boast" (Ephesians 2:8,9).

When We Receive Christ, We Experience a New Birth

(Read John 3:1–8.)

We Receive Christ By Personal Invitation

[Christ speaking] "Behold, I stand at the door and knock; if anyone hears My voice and opens the door, I will come in to him" (Revelation 3:20).

Receiving Christ involves turning to God from self (repentance) and trusting Christ to come into our lives to forgive us of our sins and to make us what He wants us to be. Just to agree intellectually that Jesus Christ is the Son of God and that He died on the cross for our sins is not enough. Nor is it enough to have an emotional experience. We receive Jesus Christ by faith, as an act of our will.

These two circles represent two kinds of lives:

Self-Directed Life
S – Self is on the throne
✝ – Christ is outside the life
● – Interests are directed by self, often resulting in discord and frustration

Christ-Directed Life
✝ – Christ is in the life and on the throne
S – Self is yielding to Christ
● – Interests are directed by Christ, resulting in harmony with God's plan

Which circle best represents your life?
Which circle would you like to have represent your life?

The following explains how you can receive Christ:

You Can Receive Christ Right Now by Faith Through Prayer
(Prayer is talking with God)

God knows your heart and is not so concerned with your words as He is with the attitude of your heart. The following is a suggested prayer:

> *Lord Jesus, I want to know You personally. Thank You for dying on the cross for my sins. I open the door of my life and receive You as my Savior and Lord. Thank You for forgiving my sins and giving me eternal life. Take control of the throne of my life. Make me the kind of person You want me to be.*

Does this prayer express the desire of your heart?

If it does, I invite you to pray this prayer right now, and Christ will come into your life, as He promised.

How to Know That Christ Is in Your Life

Did you receive Christ into your life? According to His promise in Revelation 3:20, where is Christ right now in relation to you? Christ said that He would come into your life. Would He mislead you? On what authority do you know that God has answered your prayer? (The trustworthiness of God Himself and His Word.)

The Bible Promises Eternal Life to All Who Receive Christ

"The witness is this, that God has given us eternal life, and this life is in His Son. He who has the Son has the life; he who does not have the Son of God does not have the life. These things I have written to you who believe in the name of the Son of God, in order that you may know that you have eternal life" (1 John 5:11–13).

Thank God often that Christ is in your life and that He will never leave you (Hebrews 13:5). You can know on the basis of His promise that Christ lives in you and that you have eternal life from the very moment you invite Him in. He will not deceive you.

An important reminder…

Feelings Can Be Unreliable

You might have expectations about how you should feel after placing your trust in Christ. While feelings are important, they are unreliable indicators of your sincerity or the trustworthiness of God's promise. Our feelings change easily, but God's Word and His character remain constant. This illustration shows the relationship among **fact** (God and His Word), **faith** (our trust in God and His Word), and our **feelings**.

FAITH   FEELING

FACT   FACT   FACT

Fact: The chair is strong enough to support you.
Faith: You believe this chair will support you, so you sit in it.

Feeling: You may or may not feel comfortable in this chair, but it continues to support you.

The promise of God's Word, the Bible—not our feelings —is our authority. The Christian lives by faith (trust) in the trustworthiness of God Himself and His Word.

Now That You Have Entered Into a Personal Relationship With Christ

The moment you received Christ by faith, as an act of your will, many things happened, including the following:

- Christ came into your life (Revelation 3:20; Colossians 1:27).
- Your sins were forgiven (Colossians 1:14).
- You became a child of God (John 1:12).
- You received eternal life (John 5:24).
- You began the great adventure for which God created you (John 10:10; 2 Corinthians 5:17; 1 Thessalonians 5:18).

Can you think of anything more wonderful that could happen to you than entering into a personal relationship with Jesus Christ? Would you like to thank God in prayer right now for what He has done for you? By thanking God, you demonstrate your faith.

To enjoy your new relationship with God...

Suggestions for Christian Growth

Spiritual growth results from trusting Jesus Christ. "The righteous man shall live by faith" (Galatians 3:11). A life of faith will enable you to trust God increasingly with every detail of your life, and to practice the following:

G *Go* to God in prayer daily (John 15:7).

R *Read* God's Word daily (Acts 17:11); begin with the Gospel of John.

O *Obey* God moment by moment (John 14:21).

W *Witness* for Christ by your life and words (Matthew 4:19; John 15:8).

T *Trust* God for every detail of your life (1 Peter 5:7).

H *Holy Spirit*—allow Him to control and empower your daily life and witness (Galatians 5:16,17; Acts 1:8; Ephesians 5:18).

Fellowship in a Good Church

God's Word admonishes us not to forsake "the assembling of ourselves together" (Hebrews 10:25). Several logs burn brightly together, but put one aside on the cold hearth and the fire goes out. So it is with your relationship with other Christians. If you do not belong to a church, do not wait to be invited. Take the initiative; call the pastor of a nearby church where Christ is honored and His Word is preached. Start this week, and make plans to attend regularly.

Resources

My Heart in His Hands: Renew a Steadfast Spirit Within Me. Spring—renewal is everywhere; we are reminded to cry out to God, "Renew a steadfast spirit within me." The first of four books in Vonette Bright's new devotional series, this book will give fresh spiritual vision and hope to women of all ages. ISBN 1-56399-161-6

My Heart in His Hands: Set Me Free Indeed. Summer —a time of freedom. Are there bonds that keep you from God's best? With this devotional, a few moments daily can help you draw closer to the One who gives true freedom. This is the second of four in the devotional series. ISBN 1-56399-162-4

My Heart in His Hands: Lead Me in the Way Everlasting. We all need guidance, and God is the ultimate leader. These daily moments with God will help you to rely on His leadership. The final in the four-book devotional series. ISBN 1-56399-164-0

The Joy of Hospitality: Fun Ideas for Evangelistic Entertaining. Co-written with Barbara Ball, this practical book tells how to share your faith through hosting barbecues, coffees, holiday parties, and other events in your home. ISBN 1-56399-057-1

The Joy of Hospitality Cookbook. Filled with uplifting scriptures and quotations, this cookbook contains hundreds of delicious recipes, hospitality tips, sample menus, and family traditions that are sure to make your entertaining a memorable and eternal success. Co-written with Barbara Ball. ISBN 1-56399-077-6

The Greatest Lesson I've Ever Learned. In this treasury of inspiring, real-life experiences, twenty-three prominent women of faith share their "greatest lessons." Does God have faith- and character-building lessons for you in their rich, heart-warming stories? ISBN 1-56399-085-7

Beginning Your Journey of Joy. This adaptation of the *Four Spiritual Laws* speaks in the language of today's women and offers a slightly feminine approach to sharing God's love with your neighbors, friends, and family members. ISBN 1-56399-093-8

These and other fine products from *NewLife* Publications are available from your favorite bookseller or by calling (800) 235-7255 (within U.S.) or (407) 826-2145, or by visiting www.newlifepubs.com.